another place called home

surviving foster care
a memoir
Susan DuMond

"The Visit" appeared in Fish Anthology 2013, Published in Ireland, Durrus, Bantry, Co. Cork

Print ISBN: 978-1-54394-078-7

eBook ISBN: 978-1-54394-079-4

To Mac and Miss Maude
Who helped me find strength and courage,
Who taught me to believe in myself.
I honor and esteem them.
I bow to their memory.

CONTENTS

PREFACE

The Susquehanna Valley Children's Home where I was deposited at eleven was called an orphanage but we only had one orphan. Stewart was considered the lucky one. The rest of us were consumed by our troubled and broken homes.

To us, this institution was *Another Place Called Home.* Here, our lives centered around the Main Building, a huge ancient stone structure that was scary and reeked of mystery. We lived between the shadow of the homes we left behind and the dread of where we would end up. In town, we heard the whispers, "They're from the Home."

I wrote Sue's story in the first person, present tense to bring Sue and her story closer to you, the reader. Her voice, perceptions, and experiences begin with Sue at age eleven and evolve as Sue matures. Her narrative also suggests how chaotic adolescence is when there is no parent. As some research suggests, without a close adult to help reminisce and interpret events, life is especially episodic. In the Home, we were merely what happened to us.

Sue's story concludes as she reaches eighteen, the moment when foster care ends. It's called "aging out." It's when she must leave the Home. This is an especially rough time for foster kids who have not found a placement with a family. I want you, the reader, to be by her side, to experience the evolution of her life and the finality of that horizon as she did.

Pat Schneider, a well known and highly respected author and founder of Amherst Writers and Artists, shared her experience about writing her story. Like me, Pat was placed in an orphanage at eleven. She kept diaries but, for years, did not refer to them. After she wrote *Wake Up Laughing* where she mentioned her time in the home, a woman who then ran the orphanage sent along Pat's sixth grade report card. That opened the door and she finally researched her experience and wrote her story. In *Writing Alone and with Others*, she tells us that "Until that moment, almost half a century later, I could not look at the gold in the deepest room of my childhood. Now I am writing about it."

Another Place Called Home represents the kind of achievement I wish for every child, foster kid or not. We all have the possibility of self-truth; we need to see it, hang on to it, face it, let it guide us even in the dark.

Susan DuMond

I AM ELEVEN

First night at the Home

"**G**et up! *FIRE!* All of you, on your feet!"

I wake up fast. That woman who brought me up here is yelling. A big overhead light flashes on and off. Girls run around everywhere grabbing shoes and stuff.

"Get up, get up!" the woman hollers. She scrambles through the long room, shaking the metal beds. She's tall and her back is straight. She has on an old pink robe and she scuffs like her shoes aren't tied. I remember now—she's Miss Hartford, and I'm in some building at the Home called Orton.

A girl with big glasses yanks a shirt out of a locker. "Where's the fire?" she yells.

"It's one of the new cottages. Now, *all of you*, get to the porch! And *don't dawdle!*"

I stand up so fast I get dizzy. Girls are everywhere. I look at the wall full of pink, rusty-looking lockers. Oh geez, I'm in this weird place and there's a fire? Where's the paper bag with my jeans?

When Miss Hartford flies by me, I take a deep breath and run behind her in my PJ's. Forget the jeans.

The floor feels like ice. I get to the top of the stairs and smell smoke. The air's so hot, it's like the fire is in here. My brain freezes and I taste throw-up. I don't want to heave. Swallow.

"Stay together, all of you. *I need to see you!*" Now Miss Hartford is yelling up from the bottom of the stairs. Girls push and shove so hard I can't get near the railing. A bony elbow whacks my side. I squish my way down. Nobody even looks at me. Miss Hartford stands stiff and straight like a guard. We run straight for the front door.

"Wait on the porch. *DO YOU HEAR ME?*" Boy she's so loud I want to turn away. But I keep moving. My bare feet hit the cold wooden porch.

Most of the girls bunch up at the porch railing and stare at the fire. I lean against the house. I don't know where I am. They took Mom away yesterday and put me here. Lots of orange lights flash in the sky. Swallow.

Miss Hartford hurries out on the porch. She stops right in front of me under a light that's on the porch ceiling. She looks kind of old, but I can't tell for sure. She pushes her glasses up and points her finger around like she's counting us. Her hands are shaking. I can even hear her breathing. All the girls are racing around. A loud popping sound comes from the burning building, and sparks fly up like fireworks. I make my feet stay back by the house and squeeze my legs hard to get them to stop shaking.

A siren blasts through the night. A long, red fire truck swings around the corner and makes a really fast stop right between us and the fire. The other girls push their way back to the porch railing to watch, and this time I creep up behind them and stand on tip-toe. Men in bright yellow coats jump off the truck and drag a huge black hose right up to the fire. They're shouting, but I can't tell what they're saying.

Sirens start up again. This time two police cars come around the corner really fast. The lights on top are swirling around. They screech up on the lawn right next to the porch. I see big flames beyond all the flashing lights.

Two policemen climb out of the first car and run toward the fire. They don't even close their doors. Another man gets out of the second car and hurries straight over to the porch.

I can feel Miss Hartford standing right beside me. I take a quick look. She's pinching her robe closed up by her neck. Her face looks tight, like she's mad. I look where she's looking. She's glaring at a tall thin girl pacing back and forth at the top of the front steps. She's real close to the edge of the porch. She's got a lit cigarette in her hand—I can smell it. Boy, I bet that's against the rules. She tosses her long, red-gold hair. It makes me think of a pony. Her hair is real pretty. I bet she's fifteen or sixteen. I'm eleven.

The policeman stops at the bottom of the steps. When he looks up at the girl with the cigarette, the rest of us quit moving. All I hear is water rushing through the hose.

He stares at her long and hard, then says, "She the one?" His voice is real loud. I take a quick look at Miss Hartford. She turns and looks right at the girl, then she nods.

The girl glares at the man as she flicks her cigarette over the railing. She suddenly grabs Miss Hartford by the arm and drags her over to the edge of the porch. Miss Hartford pulls back and, for a second, it looks like they're dancing. Their feet shuffle around and then the girl shoves Miss Hartford so hard she flies off the steps, her arms spinning around. Miss Hartford lands on her knees on the sidewalk. Her glasses are gone.

The girl with the pretty hair is still on the porch. She's swinging her arms and bouncing on her toes like she's showing off. Somebody behind me giggles.

The policeman bends down and helps Miss Hartford get up. He stays by her side while she brushes off her knees. When she stands up straight, he leans over and says something to her. She nods and points right at the red-gold girl. He quick turns toward us on the porch and practically jumps up the steps.

He grabs the girl by the arm and drags her down the stairs and across the yard. She yells and fights the whole time. When he gets her to the police car, he pushes her head down and folds her almost in half, shoving her into the back seat. He slams the door shut.

I step back close to the house. I lean against it, shut my eyes tight, and think about nights with Mom.

When I was seven years old, maybe even younger, sometimes I'd lie next to Mom on top of the covers. "Sue-Sue," she'd say to me in a slow voice, "Come curl up next to me like a good girl. If I know you're safe, it helps Mommy go to sleep."

I didn't dare move. If I woke her up, she'd get mad. I'd just stare into the dark and wait for her to put down her glass and fall asleep. I knew how to lie so still, so quiet, you'd think I was dead. Sometimes my leg would get all pins and needles, but I almost never turned over.

I used to think about how hard it was without a dad. Sometimes when Mom was at work, I'd get out the pictures of him. They were black and white. In the one I liked the best, he was smiling and holding a little dark-haired baby. His face was wide and his hair started up high on his forehead. In all the pictures, he wore glasses.

After a while, I open my eyes and look around the porch. It took a long time, but they got the fire out. I can smell the wet ashes. The other girls are sitting on the porch steps, huddling together to stay warm. I sit down on the top step and watch the police cars drive away. Some of them whisper together, but I stay by myself. I rub my arms and wiggle my bare feet to try to get warm. After the fire truck pulls away, Miss Hartford stands up.

"Come on, girls. It's time to go back inside." She sounds real tired.

Nobody talks and we go slow. My eyes itch, and the inside of the house smells like wet ashes. Even upstairs in the dorm I smell it. The ceiling light is off. In the dark, I find my bed and crawl in and pull the smoky sheet up over my head.

The morning after

Miss Hartford comes marching through the dorm. I bet it's really early but I don't see a clock anywhere. "This is a day the Lord hath made. Rejoice and be glad in it." She says this in a loud voice over and over as she passes our beds.

I sit up and watch girls open lockers. It takes a while, but I see there's one rusty old locker that no one touches. As soon as I go over and open it, I see my paper bag. I pull out a pair of jeans and a T-shirt. One of the girls who hardly looked at me last night during the fire pokes me in the arm. "Hurry up. We can't be late."

Miss Hartford marches past us. There's a small hole in the back of her sweater.

"Janice, show Sue where the main dining room is. And don't dawdle," she calls to the girl who poked me.

Janice makes a face. She is tall and skinny, and her dress kind of hangs on her. Up close I can smell her hair. It's stringy and kind of oily. I bet she hasn't washed it in a week, maybe even longer.

I follow her down the stairs and outside. As soon as we cross the road out front, I see where the fire was. There's a small house just a ways down our little street that's burned down on one side. Last night, they called it one of the "new cottages." I guess nobody lives there yet. I slow down. The air still smells like wet ashes.

"Hurry up," Janice hollers. I run to catch up.

"We eat in here." She points at a big stone building. It looks really old, like in a scary movie. There are five tall windows upstairs. They're close together and round at the top. They look like eyes.

Stuck on the building next to the front steps, there's a big metal sign. I stop and read it out loud. I keep my voice quiet. "Susquehanna Valley Children's Home."

Janice hears me. "Of course, silly, what else would it say?" She rolls her eyes like I'm stupid. She opens the big wooden door. I squeeze through behind her and turn my head so I don't get the sour smell from her hair.

We go down a long hallway with so many doors, I stop counting. There's hardly any light. I try not to let the rubber on the bottom of my sneakers make squeaky noises on the linoleum.

At the end of the hall, there's a sign that says "Cafeteria." Janice pushes her way in through the swinging door. I come in quick behind her.

We're in a noisy crowded room that's hot and steamy. All around us, kids are carrying trays of food. They're all talking. I hear boys' voices, too.

Janice leads me to a stack of trays and a counter where kids are sliding trays along. I see women behind the counter handing kids plates of food over some kind of glass divider. Some older girls push past Janice and me in the line.

In my head, I hear Mom's voice. "Blend in, Sue-Sue, and people won't bother you." I try to stick close to Janice, sliding my tray along behind hers.

I'm waiting for the cafeteria lady to hand me my plate when I hear the girl right behind me in line talking to someone. Her voice sounds rough.

"That crazy bitch started the fire. That means it's Goodbye, Helen."

She makes little snorting sounds. I want to see who's talking, but I don't dare turn around. I listen, but I don't hear any more. I bet the girl she calls Helen is the one who pushed Miss Hartford off the porch.

The cafeteria lady has her brown hair tucked behind her ears and covered in a net. She hands me a heavy white plate. It's got scrambled eggs and a piece of toast on it. Mostly, Mom and I have cereal in the morning. The eggs smell warm and good. When I look up at her, the lady winks at me and smiles.

I stay right behind Janice as she carries her tray and backs her way through another swinging door. It's the dining room.

There must be a hundred kids in here. Every kid I've seen so far looks taller and older than me. They're all standing next to dark wooden tables, like the ones in the library at my school. I count room for seven kids and a grown-up at each table. Nobody is sitting down.

When Janice starts for a table, I stay right next to her. As soon as we get there, I put my tray down and stand behind a chair just like she does. Miss Hartford looks like a captain at the head of the table. Out of the corner of my eye I see her fussing with a piece of silver tape on the side of her glasses. I bet they broke when she fell.

There's a gray-haired man sitting at the head of a long table at the front of the room. Nobody is up there with him. He's got glasses on, and he's reading a newspaper. He looks important in his suit and tie, like he's a school principal, or maybe a librarian. His hair is combed and neat. After the kids stop bursting into the dining room, the man stands up and buttons his jacket. Right away, the kids get quiet. The man folds his hands in front of him and bows his head. The kids all bow their heads, so I do too. It's like we're in church. I peek just a little to watch him.

When the room gets really quiet, he speaks. "Let us give thanks."

His voice is strong and clear. Somehow it sounds like he cares about things, like what we do here matters. "Bless this food that we are about to receive and make us truly thankful. Amen." Except sometimes when Mom sent me to Sunday School, I never heard grace like this.

When a hundred kids pull out their chairs, it makes a real loud scraping noise. It gets quiet again as soon as we start eating, just the sounds of silverware clinking on the plates and at least a hundred kids eating eggs and toast and slurping milk.

I want to know about the man who said grace.

"Who is he?" I whisper to Janice.

"That's Mac. He's in charge." She loads her fork up with eggs and sticks it in her mouth.

After breakfast, we go back to Orton. I sit on the couch next to a girl named Donna, who doesn't seem to mind. I heard her talk to her sister, Ellen, at breakfast and they seemed okay. They are the only two black girls I've seen at the Home. Donna's taller than I am, and I bet she's older, too.

After a while I get up my nerve. "The girl who started the fire. Is her name Helen?"

Donna turns and stares at me. "Yeah. How'd you know?" Her eyes are dark brown and shiny behind her big round glasses.

I shrug. "What happened to her?"

Donna keeps her voice low. "The cops took her to the infirmary. The nurse locked her up for the night." She looks around at the other girls in the room to see if anyone is paying attention. "They came back real early this morning and took her away. I saw them from the dorm window. Handcuffs and everything. No sirens." She shakes her head and kind of snorts. "Boy, she looked really pissed."

"Where did they take her?" I whisper.

Donna looks at me with her huge brown eyes. "She got sent up."

We lock eyes. I nod like I understand, but I don't.

The last day I saw Mom

The dorm is empty except for me. I sit on my bed and look out the window. I keep thinking about yesterday, the last day I saw Mom.

She always worried when I was gone, even if I wasn't late coming home. And yesterday I was a little late. I'd gone swimming in the big public pool, the one with the slide at En-Joie Park. I liked to pretend I was Esther Williams. Boy I loved to watch her swim in the movies. Anyway, I knew I was late, so I was hurrying home.

As I opened the outside door to our big old apartment building, I smelled cigarettes and cabbage soup, like always. But yesterday, I heard loud voices coming from the second floor. I stopped at the bottom of the steps. That's where Mom and I lived. There were only two apartments up there, and ours was in the back. These were men's voices, and there weren't any men living upstairs. Just Mrs. Karnitsky and her kids in the front, and Mom and me in the back. I stood in the dark hall, listening. It was so hot, sweat ran down the side of my face. I sopped it up with the towel that was wrapped around my new red bathing suit.

I waited for maybe a minute, but when the voices didn't stop, I figured I'd better go upstairs. I climbed the steps and opened the door to our apartment. We only had two rooms, the front room and the kitchen. Nobody was in the front room. I could hear people moving around in the kitchen and then cupboard doors started banging. I tiptoed as far as the doorway to look in. The kitchen was crowded. There were a couple of policemen and two ladies. Mom was sitting at the little wooden table where we ate. Nobody paid attention to me, at least not right away.

Mom had her legs crossed, and she was jiggling her foot. Her jelly glass, the one she used all the time, was right in front of her.

When a policeman started shoving things around inside our cupboards, I looked over at Mom, but she didn't say anything. Another cop, an older one with hardly any hair, was standing by the window. He was peering down into the back alley. What were these two cops looking for? Why were they here?

The two ladies stayed over beside the window. They kept whispering to each other. They had on flowered dresses.

"Ma'am?" It was the younger policeman talking. He looked at Mom. "Uh, Mrs. Pickering, ma'am?" He sounded like he was still in school. "Ma'am, are you drinking alcohol?"

I stared at Mom. She is small and thin, with tiny ankles and wrists. I've always wanted to look like her someday, with golden eyes and tan skin. Even in winter, she looks like she's just come in from the sun. My eyes are brown, but Mom says they are really hazel, which is sort of like hers. Her hair is brown, and it's short and wavy. Mine is straight and dark brown, and it touches my shoulders. Sometimes at night before Mom and I go to sleep, she lets me brush her hair while we count out loud to a hundred.

When the policeman asked her about drinking alcohol, Mom sat up straight and stuck her chin out. She held on tight to the jelly glass.

"No officer," she said. I watched her put on a fake smile. "I am not drinking alcohol."

My hand flew up and covered my mouth. For sure, Mom was not telling the truth. The two cops pulled her up out of her chair and dragged her to the back door. They were going to take Mom down the rickety back stairs that were supposed to be a fire escape. The jelly glass crashed on the floor and brown stuff spilled out. She tried to push the men away. I started yelling "Mom! Mom!" and stamping my feet. One of the ladies grabbed me by the arm and shook her head, like she was telling me "No."

There was a lot of banging as they pulled Mom out the back door and down the outside stairs. I pushed past the ladies so I could see out the kitchen window.

That's when I saw the ambulance in the alley. The back doors were wide open. Mom twisted and squirmed a lot, but she's so small they just lifted her up and put her inside. She was yelling, but I couldn't tell what she was saying. One policeman slammed the doors shut. The lights flashed and the siren started as the ambulance began to drive up the alley. The policemen walked behind it.

Soon the kitchen was quiet. I bit my lip hard to keep from crying. I'd never been left alone without Mom.

One of the ladies walked over and put her hand on my shoulder.

"We need to pack a few things for you, dear. Clothes. And pajamas. Do you have a suitcase?"

I shook my head. I pulled out a paper bag from the kitchen cupboard, and the lady watched as I put some T-shirts and jeans in it.

"Where are we going?" My voice sounded like it was far away, like it wasn't me.

"First, we'll get some supper. Then we'll figure things out."

I stopped putting T-shirts in the bag and stared at them.

"Where did they take my mom?"

They glanced at each other. One lady shrugged and said, "Don't worry. She'll be all right."

Her dress was cream-colored and sprinkled with pale pink and blue morning glories. The other lady's dress was lavender and had lots of bright yellow and orange flowers. The cream-colored lady was the one who talked to me. The lavender lady mostly wrote things down.

When we left, I locked the apartment door like I'm supposed to. I put the key in my blue jeans pocket. Then I followed them down the front stairs with my paper bag.

We went to a place called the Baptist Bible Seminary to have supper in their cafeteria. It seemed weird to be eating at a Bible school. I brought my paper bag inside and kept it on a chair next to me.

"What about your Uncle Bob and Aunt Lillian?" the lavender lady asked me. "Could you stay with them again for a while, do you suppose?"

I shook my head no and stared at my sandwich. I didn't want to talk about the last time we stayed there. Mom got into a fight with Uncle Bob, who is her brother, and we had to leave.

"Do you have other relatives nearby?" This time it was the cream-colored lady. She smiled a lot. Her eyes were the same blue as the flowers on her dress.

"No, ma'am."

That's when the lavender lady started talking about a place called the Home. I watched her large round arms and tried to pay attention.

"You won't have your own room, of course—you'll sleep in a big room with the other girls in Orton. That's the name of the girls' residence. But you'll have your own locker for your things." She was trying to sound cheerful. "I think you'll like it there."

Sleep in a room with a bunch of girls? Yuck. I'd always just been with Mom. But now Mom was gone. I bit my lip.

"I don't think it will be for long." It was the cream-colored lady. Her voice was soft. "Your mother will be well again soon, I'm sure."

Be well? What did that mean?

We cleared our plates and walked out of the cafeteria at the Bible Seminary. They drove me straight to the Home. By then, it was dark. They left me with Miss Hartford. Right away she took me upstairs and told me to put my bag in a locker. She had me put on my pajamas. Then she pointed to a bed, and I got in it. I cried myself to sleep. Later, she woke us up because of the fire.

Too many questions

It's almost time for lights-out. Miss Hartford's in the big soft chair reading her Bible. She's done this every night since I got here. That was four days ago. I'm sitting right across from her on the edge of the couch. I want to ask her what happened to Mom, but I don't know how to talk to her. It's like she's the principal of a school or something, but it's "The Home," not school. I already asked about that because I love school. It's a safe place.

I watch her while she reads. Her mouth is in a thin line and her forehead is wrinkled, like she's thinking hard. She keeps touching the tape on the side of her glasses. I sit up straight and smooth my skirt down over my knees.

"Miss Hartford?" I wait until she looks at me. I want to see her eyes. "Why did they take my mom away?"

She closes the Bible, but she keeps her finger in it. I can hear water running upstairs in the shower.

"Do you remember your neighbor, Mrs. Karnitsky?"

I nod. It was her cabbage soup that made the whole hallway in our old building smell yucky. I saw her and her two kids come and go sometimes. And boy, I heard the kids yelling in the hall. I never saw Mr. Karnitsky.

Miss Hartford turns away and looks out the window. The porch outside is dark.

"Well, Sue," she says, and turns back to me. "I was told that she called the police."

My stomach starts to hurt.

"Why? Why would she do that?"

"Well, dear, you see…" Miss Hartford's eyes are dark. "You know the little Karnitsky boy?"

"Uh huh," I say. I don't tell her, but he cries a lot and his nose runs. Mom said I could babysit for him after I turned 12 if Mrs. Karnitsky wanted me to. I figured she did. She always smiled at me and patted me on the shoulder.

"Well, Mrs. Karnitsky told the police that your mother threatened to throw the boy off the second-story porch if he didn't stop screaming."

I stare at Miss Hartford. Is she telling the truth?

I stand up fast. "My mother wouldn't do that! She'd never hurt that little boy!" My voice is so loud, I scare myself. I run to the other side of the sitting room and stare out the window. I'm confused. Did Mom really do this?

"Well, dear, the welfare workers who brought you here told me your mother had been drinking…"

I turn fast and run up the stairs. I don't stop to talk to any of the girls. I don't even put on my pajamas. I just climb into my lumpy bed and pull the stupid old blanket over my head.

There's something Mom used to say to me in her special voice, the one she used when I was upset and afraid. "Be sure and watch out for yourself, Sue-Sue," she'd say. "Remember, you are my big strong girl."

I dig my thumbnail into my finger to keep from crying. I think about the ladies who brought me here the other night. I bet they told Miss Hartford about my mom.

Where did they take her? Why did they bring me here?

I squirm way down under the blanket and turn on my side. I pull my knees up and curl into a ball.

Sundays

"My mom's coming to get me!" It's Janice. She's dancing around the dorm rubbing on lipstick, which isn't allowed. I'm sitting on my bed watching a bunch of girls get ready to go out for the afternoon.

I've been here almost three months and every Sunday it's like this. As soon as we get back to Orton after a really long sermon at the Baptist church, girls rush around so they're prepared to go out with their mom or dad or somebody. I don't go anywhere. I still don't even know where my mom is.

After a while, I wander down to the sitting room and look out the window. There goes Janice, skipping down the front sidewalk beside her mom. I look away.

So far, I don't mind Sundays so much. That's when some of the tough girls are gone, and Orton is quiet. Some of the girls, especially the older ones, want to beat me up. It's like they need to prove they're better than I am. A few girls in the dorm like to come after me. It's not all of them. Once, around time for lights-out, three of these girls made a tight circle around me and started pushing me and calling me bad names. I yelled and tried to make them stop, but they just laughed. They only broke the circle when we heard Miss Hartford coming up the stairs. Boy, if she wasn't around, I bet I'd be black and blue all over.

I take a long look around the sitting room. Mom and I lived in lots of different places, but we never had a big room like this. All the chairs and couches are shoved back against the walls. It looks like a waiting room at the dentist. There are some pictures from magazines on the walls. Girls sometimes rip them out and stick them up with thumbtacks. I plunk down on one of the couches and look around. There's a bright green chalkboard on one wall. It's big, like they have in school. It even has a tray across the bottom with pieces of chalk and an eraser. Across from the chalkboard, there's a tall wooden piano. Sometimes Miss Hartford plays it but only for hymns. I bet she's the only one who's allowed to use it.

I lean back on the couch and think about Sundays when I was with Mom. Most of the time, Sunday was great. Sometimes Mom would let me stay up past my bedtime, even though it was a school night. I'd help her fix supper, and we'd carry our plates into the other room. That's where we listened to the radio. I loved how the light inside it glowed in the dark.

I'd sit next to Mom and we'd listen to scary programs like "The Green Hornet" or "The Shadow." Whenever I heard the Shadow laugh, I'd shiver a little and scoot over close to Mom. Or we'd giggle at funny shows like Jack Benny. I always tried not to spill my supper on the rug. It was my job to clean up whenever we had to move, which happened a lot.

Some Sundays, instead of listening to the radio, Mom would pretend she was different people. It was like she was in the movies. Lots of times, I'd ask for my favorite.

"Mom, do the man with the little hat, the one who walks like a duck!"

"You mean Charlie Chaplin?"

Mom would straighten her back and make her legs stiff. Then she'd point her toes out and walk around the room. Her eyebrows would shoot up and she'd make her eyes big and round. Sometimes she'd even draw a tiny mustache with her eyebrow pencil. I'd clap and start laughing.

"Mom, get the jacket!" I'd holler.

She'd come back from our closet wearing a little black jacket and a black hat that was round on top. I loved watching Mom pull at the lapels with both hands as she marched around the room.

I give a big sigh, push up from the couch, and head for the piano. The white keys have brown marks on the edges. One is missing. I sit down on the bench and tap a key. It's really loud. I scoot the bench up close to the piano so I can play "Chopsticks." It's the only song I know on the piano. I pound the keys and sing along.

Dah-dah-dah-dah-dah-dah,

Dah-dah-dah-dah-dah-dah—.

Somebody grabs my shoulder. My hands fly up in the air and I nearly fall off the bench.

"Susan Pickering!" Uh oh, it's Miss Hartford. "Sunday is God's day. It is the day we go to church and honor our Lord. It is *not* a day to play 'Chopsticks' on the piano. There are rules. You should know that by now."

"Yes, Miss Hartford." I look down at the floor and make a face.

"Instead of enjoying Sunday dinner, young lady, you will do something to help you remember that you girls do *not* play around on the piano, especially on Sunday."

She grabs my arm and steers me across the room until we are standing in front of the chalkboard. She picks up a piece of chalk and in large round letters she writes, "I will not play the piano on Sunday." Then she turns around and gives me a pinched-up look before she marches out of the room. "And don't go anywhere," she announces over her shoulder.

I stare at her handwriting. The big round O's look like my sixth grade teacher's writing from last year. When Miss Hartford comes back, she's carrying one of those school composition notebooks with a black and white cover.

"Do you see that phrase?" She points at the words on the chalkboard.

"Yes, Miss Hartford," I answer. Holy cow, of course I see that phrase!

She picks my left hand up and puts the notebook in it. Then she takes a pencil out of her sweater pocket and slaps that in my other hand. "I want you to write it in here 100 times." I stare at these things and make a face, but not a big one. I don't want to have to write this 200 times.

"This is an important lesson for you, Susan. I expect you to be done writing by the time I get back from Sunday dinner." She turns and heads for the door, her face grim, her back straight. As the door closes behind her, I stick out my tongue.

After a while, I open the notebook and turn the pages. Boy, there's a lot of writing in there.

"I will not spit on the sidewalk."

"I will not take the Lord's name in vain."

"I will not swear at the housemothers."

I make a big groan. No Sunday dinner. I turn to a clean page and start writing.

The visit

I hear footsteps starting up the stairs. I can tell it's Miss Hartford. Her feet make a heavy sound. The footsteps stop.

"Sue," she calls out. "Are you up there?"

I'm sitting cross-legged on my bed reading about different countries in my favorite seventh-grade Social Studies book. I love looking at the maps. I love the school I go to. I sigh and stick my pencil in the book to keep my place.

"Yes, Miss Hartford?"

"Would you come down here, please?"

I hope I haven't done anything wrong, but there are so many rules at this place, I can't be sure. I leave my book on my bed and head down the stairs.

Even though it's November and it's cold outside, she has on the same Sunday dress as always, with little blue flowers on it. But she has her old gray cardigan on over it. Today, I took off my special dress I wear to church and put on my jeans. I'm not going anywhere.

Miss Hartford sits down in the middle of the couch and places her Bible on her lap. After she gets settled, she looks up at me and pats the cushion next to her. I pretend I don't see her do this. If I'm in trouble, I want to be standing up.

"I couldn't tell you this before, dear, but your mother has been very . . . ill." She looks at me. I don't move. I don't say anything. This is the first time Miss Hartford's said anything about my mother, except when she told me about Mom and Mrs. Karnitsky's little boy. Why is she doing this now?

Miss Hartford fusses with a button on her sweater. "Ever since you came here six months ago, she's been in a special . . . hospital."

My heart pumps so fast, it scares me. "Is she sick?"

"She's getting better now."

I stare at the floor. "Is she still in there? In that hospital?"

She shakes her head. "Not anymore."

I wait.

"Your mother is out now."

I can hardly breathe. It's like everything's frozen inside me. I turn and run to the window. I stare out at the snow. What was wrong with Mom? Do they know about how she gets sometimes?

I turn away from the window and look over at Miss Hartford. She's still sitting on the couch. Her hands are folded and her feet are crossed at the ankles. She has a big smile, like she's about to tell me something really good. But it doesn't feel that way to me. If Mom's sick, why is Miss Hartford smiling? I almost don't want to know.

"Your mother is coming to see you, Sue. She's coming to take you out for a visit." She holds out a crumpled piece of white paper. "Here's your pass. When she gets here, you can leave the grounds for an hour."

I walk over and take it. It has three signatures, just like the other girls' passes.

"Today?" I ask. My voice is small.

Miss Hartford nods.

"When?"

No answer.

"How soon?"

She looks at her watch.

"Not long." She gives me a small smile and uncrosses her feet as she gets ready to stand. "Oh, and she's bringing your stepfather with her."

My stepfather? I don't have a stepfather.

I look out the window at the gray icy day.

Some nights, Mom would yell and carry on about my father, swearing and calling him bad names. I remember one night when she'd had a lot to drink. She'd been crying and smoking and complaining for a long time. That was one of the nights she came after me. Her cheeks were bright red, and her eyes had turned dark. It was almost bedtime and we were in the room where we slept.

Mom was holding the hairbrush in her hand. The brush part was soft. The back was made of thick, dark wood. That's the part I saw when she came toward me. When she raised her arm up high, I got sick inside.

Right away, I jumped into our big chair and rolled myself into a ball. I pulled my knees tight up to my chest. I hid my face with my hands and squeezed my eyes shut. I'd done this before.

When the back of the brush smacked my hand, the little bone that sticks out by my wrist started throbbing like a toothache.

"You look just like him, goddamn it. Filthy bastard. YOU LOOK JUST LIKE HIM!"

I yanked my hand away and got myself turned over so I could bury my face in the cushion.

The brush banged hard on my back a lot of times, more times than I could count. It hurt so much.

After a while, I heard Mom crying and breathing really loud. I looked between my fingers as she kicked off her shoes and curled up on the couch. After a while the brush fell to the floor by her shoes.

I crawled out of the chair and slipped into my bed. I turned out the light and pulled the sheet up over me. My hand was throbbing so much I stuck it under the pillow.

In the morning the hairbrush was still on the floor. In the next room, I heard the coffee pot bubbling. There was the sound of the icebox door opening then closing.

My back was stiff and sore. My hand was puffy on the back near the little bone. It hurt when I poked it. How would I know if it was broken? I poked some more.

I slid out of bed and went into the kitchen.

"Morning, Sue-Sue," Mom said. She was pouring a cup of coffee. A cigarette was burning in the ashtray on the kitchen table. The bottle was gone.

"Cereal?" she asked.

"Okay." I walked past her into the bathroom and closed the door. I stood on tiptoe and turned so I could see my back in the mirror. There was a reddish blue mark, sort of like a horseshoe. I looked at my hand. There was a blue spot next to the bone. I splashed water on my face and brushed my teeth. Then I got my school clothes out of our closet and got dressed.

Back in the kitchen, I ate my cereal and watched her, but not while she was looking. She smiled at me and reached over to smooth my hair. When I looked in her eyes, I could tell she didn't remember.

As I stand by the window, a big dark-colored car drives up to the porch. It has four doors. We never had a car. Mom is in the passenger seat, and a man is driving the car. The man gets out and hurries around the car to help Mom get out. He holds her arm as they move slowly along the icy sidewalk. This "stepfather" man is tall. He's hunched over a little in his heavy jacket and his dark gray hat, the kind with a brim. When he glances up, I see he has glasses. They're beige like his face. Mom has a tight grip on his arm. She looks small, smaller than before.

As soon as they start up the front steps to the porch, I open the door. I already have my coat on. I don't want Miss Hartford to come over and meet my Mom.

When the man takes off his hat, I recognize him. His name is Les. He used to live downstairs in our building. I knew his wife, too, before she died. Her name was Mamie. I think he's nice, but I can't really remember. He seems to understand that I don't want them to come inside. He turns Mom around on the sidewalk to go back to the car.

"Well, where do you want to go, Sue?" Les asks. By now I'm climbing into the back seat of his car.

"There's a soda shop down by the junior high." I point down Home Avenue. He starts the car. I look out the window and listen to the sound of the engine as Les drives us away.

He parks in front of Tony the Greek's. We go in and sit in a booth. The windows are steamy and you can't see outside. Hardly anybody is in here, just two men in another booth drinking what looks like beer. Mom sits next to Les. He lights her cigarette first and then his. When she turns her head, I see gray in her hair. Geez, being here after all this time with Mom and a new stepfather is so weird, I don't know what to say. Why didn't Miss Hartford tell me earlier?

"What would you like to have, Sue?" he asks.

I order a soda. Mom and Les have coffee.

"How about a hamburger?" It's mom asking. "Are you hungry?"

I shake my head.

After a while, it gets warm and we take off our coats. Les is wearing a short-sleeved shirt. He sees me staring at the little half-moon scars mixed with the gray hairs on the outside of his arms.

"I get these from the hot metal in the factory where I work," he says, rubbing his arm. "Sometimes little pieces fly off and burn you." He smiles like this is just something that happens.

Mom tells me she got out of the hospital a month ago, and that's when she and Les got married. They're renting a new place.

"Sue-Sue, I miss you so much," she says. She is real thin but her eyes are clear.

"I didn't know where you were," I tell her. My voice is quiet.

"It's just as well." She looks at Les.

"We hope you'll come and live with us real soon," he says. He puts his arm around Mom's shoulders. "You'll have your own room, too. Right, Peg?" He gives Mom a squeeze. Her face is wet with tears. I don't know what to say, so I don't say anything.

On our way back, Les drives slowly. Mom sits beside him, smoking. I'm in the back. Les comes to a stop right in front of Orton. He turns to look at me over his shoulder.

"Sue, these last several months have been hard on you, I know. But we'll try to make up for it." His voice is quiet.

I nod, but I don't know what that means. I quick get out of the car. I don't want Mom to have to walk on the ice again. She rolls down her window, and I lean in and kiss her on the cheek. "Thanks, Mom," I tell her. I don't know why I say this.

I walk around to Les's side and stand by the open window. I can feel the warm air from the heater even from here.

"Be good," he says. I nod and start down the walk. When I get inside, I look out the sitting room window. The car is still there. I wave. They wave back. I watch Les drive away.

Figure it out

As soon as I get back from school the next day, I pull on my jeans and grab my pea coat and boots. As usual, all our mittens, scarves, and hats are in a pile on the floor of the coat closet. That's where I almost always find my gloves, the ones that are warm and fuzzy. As I put them on, I can almost hear Miss Hartford telling me to "take better care of your things, Sue." I make a face. She says that a lot.

I pull the front door shut behind me and turn left, down the little hill. Even though it's cold and snowy and gray outside, it feels good to be by myself. It's nice not have a lot of people around. Noisy girls make it hard to think. And this way, I don't have to worry about what they might do to me.

I stop on the sidewalk that runs by the new cottages. They look sort of done to me, like they're almost ready for us kids to move in. I wonder when that will be. And what that will be like.

Here's the one that almost burned down. I can tell by the pile of blackish wood and pieces of cinder block piled right beside it. It looks like it's almost fixed now after so many months. That night, my first night here last summer, was bad.

I walk some more and rub my hands on my cheeks to warm up my face.

What if I end up in one of the cottages? Would that be okay? Or what if I get sent home to that new place where Mom and Les live? I stop walking. Figuring out what I want is scary. What if I don't want to be with Mom and Les?

I bet I don't get to say anything about this anyway.

I stare at the row of cottages. Except for the dirty snow piled up around them, they could be in a magazine. They're kind of square, but they have an upstairs and a downstairs. There's some red brick going around the bottom. Miss Hartford told us there's going to be only twelve girls in a cottage, and some of us would get to have only one roommate. Boy, I hope if I'm here, I get to live in the same cottage as Donna. She's the only one I really talk to. Donna doesn't tell on me or laugh at me or anything.

I trudge across the gray snow and look through the front windows. I bet that's the living room. There's even a fireplace. It's weird looking at these new houses when everything else here is old. I mean *really* old. I turn and look up the little hill at the Main Building. That place where we eat and where Mac has his office is so gray and spooky.

I kick some snow along the sidewalk in front of the new cottages. Which one would I get to live in? And which girls would I be with? Some of them in the dorm like to fight so much, I never look them in the eye for fear they'll turn on me. Some of them already have. They even stand on the toilet in the ladies room in the church basement and blow their cigarette smoke out a little window by the ceiling. Donna says most of the really rough girls will end up in reform school, the place where they sent Helen, but for now, they like to pick on girls like me.

I wander past the rest of the cottages and think about Mom. Yesterday, she said she wants me to come live with her. And with Les. I miss her a lot, but it kind of scares me, going back. What if she's not really well, whatever that means? What if she still drinks a lot and gets mad and comes after me with a hairbrush? And now Les is there. What does *that* mean?

Oh, hell, I whisper to myself and stamp my boots along the snowy walkway. I giggle and make a snowball and toss it at the big tree in front of one of the cottages. I'd be locked in a closet for the next month if Miss Hartford ever heard me say "hell" out loud.

Maybe she'd make me write a thousand times, "I'll never say 'hell' out loud." I stick my tongue out, just for practice.

I start up the sidewalk toward the Main Building. If I go home, that means I'll have to change schools again. So far, I really like the school I go to. It's only a couple of blocks away. My Social Studies teacher, Mr. Cicak, even brings his own orange juice to class and drinks it while we're all talking about the big map of the world. It hangs over the blackboard behind his chair. Even thinking about this makes me smile. But what if I'm living with Mom? Where do I go to school then?

I plunk down on an old wooden bench and think some more about school. It's always been my safe place. I made a list once. I saved it, hid it in my locker. It has the names of the fourteen schools I went to before I came to the Home. I can't even say for sure what grades I finished. Or where. Mom and I moved around a lot. We never seemed to have enough money to pay the rent.

When I make my way past the windows of the Main Building, I think about Mac and the times when he's in his office. He walked with me once from the Main Building across the grounds to Orton. He asked about school and stuff, like most grownups do. But he looked me in the eye. I liked that a lot. I don't worry about him lying to me. And his eyes sort of twinkle, like they have a light behind them. Their blue color is really cool, too. Anyway, I think maybe he cares about me. He's almost a dad.

I turn and kick my way through the snow back to Orton.

Girl, age 12

When Miss Hartford comes marching through the dorm, I pull the sheet over my face.

"Rise and shine, girls," she chants.

Holy cow. It's only 6:30, and it's Christmas morning.

"We have a special treat! We're all going to have Christmas breakfast in the Gymnasium!"

The Gymnasium? She calls it that but to us, it's the Gym.

"And wear something nice. Not jeans, for heaven's sake. Something presentable. Now let's get going." She claps her hands. She does this a lot when she wants us to hurry up. "We don't want to keep the Masons waiting." I look out from under the sheet at Donna, on the next bed. "Who are the Masons?" Donna shrugs like she doesn't know either.

I slide off the bed. The floor is cold. I bet the heat isn't even turned on yet. I paw around in my locker until I find a skirt that's not too wrinkled and a sweater that almost matches. Pretty soon, we're all downstairs and bunched up in front of the window.

After a while, a car drives by. It's going so slow, it looks like it's in a funeral. Then another one comes along. Pretty soon, there's a bunch of cars in front of the Gym. The sitting room gets real quiet. Janice squeezes in close to me and pokes me in the ribs. I can tell she washed her hair. "Look," she whispers. "They brought presents."

Wow, presents! That makes me think about the one I got for Donna.

When I picked Donna's name out of the basket, I was pretty excited. I got to buy something for my friend! Miss Hartford had herded us together and taken us shopping at Woolworths so we could buy our Secret Santa gifts. "Don't spend more than $1," she told us. Well, that's all she gave us anyway, so I don't know why she had to remind us.

I already knew what Donna wanted. When we were in Woolworths after school one day, she had opened a bottle of perfume and sniffed. Then she sniffed again. Her eyes got really big. "This is for me," she whispered and started to slip it into her jacket pocket. "Don't steal it," I warned her, "or you'll get some kind of detention over Christmas." We looked at each other. She made a face and put the bottle back on the dusty shelf.

So I got Donna her own blue bottle of Evening in Paris perfume. Before they wrapped it up, I asked, "Can I smell it?" The lady behind the counter smiled and nodded. I unscrewed the top and gave it a whiff, just like Donna had done. It sure smelled pretty. I hoped she'd let me put some on once in a while.

We're still in front of the window, watching people carry presents into the Gym when the phone rings. Miss Hartford hurries across the sitting room to pick it up.

"Mer-ry Christ-mas," she says. It's like she's singing. "Oh yes, Mr. McPherson, they're all ready." She smiles at us. "Yes, sir. We'll be right over."

I put on my pea coat and rubber boots and hurry outside with the other girls. Some of them are already running to the Gym. I walk fast with Donna.

In the middle of the Gym, there's a giant Christmas tree. It's as tall as the basketball hoop. I can smell it. It smells green, like it's still alive in the forest. There are little twinkling lights and big red and green glass balls everywhere. There's even fake snow on the branches. I look at it for a long time. Mom and I never had a real Christmas tree.

Why don't I get to see Mom this Christmas? Is she "sick" again? I try not to think about it. She called the dorm a few times after her visit, but it's tough to talk with all the girls hanging around. I've always spent Christmas with Mom.

I remember one year when I got a present for her. I think I was eight. I walked all by myself in the ice and slush to the department store where she used to work. When I finally got there, I grabbed a shopping bag off the hook on my way in.

"Jingle Bells" was playing. I watched a woman go by pushing her cart. There was a Raggedy Ann doll flopped on top of lots of other stuff. I slid along on the wet floor like I was skating.

First, I found a kitchen towel with red flowers on it. They made it look like Christmas. Then I picked out a blouse with little pieces of lace on the collar. After a while, they started playing "O Little Town of Bethlehem." It was my favorite, so I sang along.

On the next aisle, there were rows of lions and tigers and horses with stripes. They looked like they were made of stone. I picked up a little brown elephant and ran my finger along his side. He was so smooth and his eyes shone and his trunk pointed way up in the air. Something made me pat him on the head and laugh. So I put him in my bag for Mom.

I wanted to get my presents to Mom right away. It was only Christmas Eve, but I couldn't wait. I pulled the shopping bag out of its hiding place in our closet and dragged it in front of Mom. She looked surprised.

"Where did this come from, Sue-Sue?"

"I got it at the store. You know, the store where you used to work?"

"The department store?" Her eyes were big. "You went there by yourself?"

"Uh huh. And they had bags right by the door like I remembered, so I got one! And wait till you see what I got you." I nudged the bag closer.

Mom started to reach inside.

"How did you pay for this?" she asked. It was her quiet voice.

"Pay for this? I brought it home for you, that's all." I looked in her eyes.

"This doesn't belong to us, honey, unless we pay for it. Do you understand that?"

I looked down. I went right by the line at the cash register. I didn't have any money.

"Oh, honey," Mom said. "This is so beautiful. Did you pick this out?"

I looked up. She was holding the elephant. I nodded.

"I have an idea, Sue-Sue. We'll go back to the store right after Christmas and pay for this wonderful elephant and return all the rest." She looked into my eyes. "Would that be okay?"

I was frozen for a minute, afraid and embarrassed.

"I'm sorry. I did a bad thing," I mumbled. I felt so bad that we had to take things back.

"You picked a beautiful gift, Sue-Sue. We'll explain everything to the manager. I know he'll understand. We'll pay for this wonderful elephant and make it all okay."

The Gym is packed full of people. Two women I've never seen before are stacking presents under the tree. A man goes by with a big smile and a tray of cocoa and doughnuts. I look around for Mac. I see him in the middle of the crowd near the tree, talking to a tall man. There's so much noise in this big room, the man has to lean down to hear what Mac says. When they laugh and nod together, it makes me smile. Mac's cheeks are red, and he has on a red and green plaid vest.

After a while, Mac goes to a little table next to the tree and rings a bell. The whole room gets quiet, just like in the dining room when we say grace.

"Boys and girls, we have a lot to be thankful for this year. We're very fortunate that the Masons and their families are here to help us celebrate Christmas." His voice is strong. It's almost like he's preaching. Then Mac explains that the Masons are men who belong to a club, and their club chose us for their "holiday project." I look around. It must be a big club.

Mac grins up at the tall man. "And we certainly hope they'll make this an annual event. Now, if you'll form a girls' line and a boys' line, it's time to see what Santa brought for each of you."

Right away, the kids are cheering. Over the crowd, I see Miss Hartford waving her arm at us. She wants us girls to line up behind her. The bigger girls push their way to the front. I end up near the back.

After what seems like forever, I get to the front of the line. A gray-haired woman who looks like she's somebody's grandmother is there to greet us. She's wearing a pin with a Santa Claus face. She wipes her hands on her apron and smiles at me.

"Merry Christmas," she says.

"Merry Christmas."

"And what's your name?"

"Sue," I tell her. "My name is Sue Pickering." I speak up. It's loud in here, and I want her to hear my name so she can find my present.

"How old are you, Sue?"

"I'm 12." Then I add, "And a half."

She moves the boxes around, reading labels. I wait. It takes a long time. Finally she holds up a box that's covered in red and gold paper.

"This is for you, Sue. Merry Christmas."

"Thank you." I take it and run to one of the empty folding chairs.

I sit down and hold tight to my package. All around me, kids are ripping the wrapping paper and opening boxes, yelling back and forth to each other. I just sit and keep my package close to me. After a while, I turn it over so I can read the tag. I want to be sure it's for me. Under the shiny red bow, the tag says, "Girl, age 12."

Going home

It's early January when Miss Hartford calls me to come downstairs to the sitting room. As soon as I walk in, I see a faded brown suitcase sitting on the floor in the center of the room. Miss Hartford is standing beside it with her arms crossed.

"Well, Sue, today's the day," she says. "You're going home to live."

My mouth drops open. When she called upstairs for me, I thought it was because I'd left my book for English class on the couch. She leans down and picks up the suitcase by its handle.

"Your mother and stepfather are already on their way."

She hands me the suitcase.

"You can use this."

She turns and walks away. Her shoulders are straight like always.

"Today? Miss Hartford?" I want her to tell me more. "Does Mac know? I mean—"

"Of course." She looks over her shoulder. "He signed the papers. Good luck, Sue."

I watch her leave. The Home doesn't tell me anything. Mom and Les didn't even come to see me at Christmas, but now, all of a sudden, I'm going to live with them?

I pick up the old suitcase and go upstairs. The plastic handle sticks to my palm. I bang open the door to my locker and start stuffing my shoes and sneakers and everything I can fit into the suitcase.

Donna is curled up on her bed looking through a teen magazine. She likes to read about what to wear on a movie date and how to attract boys, even though that kind of stuff never happens here.

"What's up?" she asks.

"After six months I'm being sent home," I tell her. My voice is flat.

"Jesus," she says and slips off her bed. "Is this good?"

I shrug my shoulders.

"Did you know about it?"

I shake my head.

"Sue?"

I turn around and look at her. Donna's eyes are the biggest I've ever seen them. My eyes are dry, but I feel lots of crying starting inside.

"I'm so confused. I feel like *hell*," I tell her. She sighs and gives me a long hug.

I stand by the big window in the sitting room and watch the road. The old brown suitcase is by my feet. I've got on my pea coat, and my fuzzy gloves are in my pocket. I hope I'm ready for this.

Mom and Les drive up in his big gray car. Mom stays in her seat, smoking. I open the front door for Les, and he reaches for the suitcase.

"Is this everything?" he asks.

"Uh huh."

He carries the suitcase out to the car and puts it in the trunk. He pats me on the shoulder, and I climb into the back seat, just like I did when they came here to see me. As he pulls away from Orton, I turn around and look out the back window. I can see Donna waving to me from the sitting room. I wave back, but I don't think she sees me. My stomach feels like a big knot.

Les doesn't say much, but Mom keeps talking, mostly about where they live. She sounds nervous.

"We have half a house, Sue-Sue. It's called a duplex. There's lots of room. We live on one side, and there's another family like ours on the other."

Another family like ours? What does that mean?

And how did this happen so fast? Why didn't anybody talk to me about it?

I watch the houses and then the stores go by as Les drives us wherever we're going.

"Where is it? The duplex?"

Mom turns around. "It's in Johnson City. Not too far from where we used to live." She reaches into the back seat to pat me on the knee.

The duplex is a regular old two-story house with a wide porch, but it has two front doors. Mom opens one, and I follow her inside. Les brings in my suitcase, then he disappears up the stairs.

Right near the door there's a big wooden radio with a curved top. It looks a lot like the one Mom and I had in our last apartment. I look over at Mom, and she's smiling.

Along one wall, there's a brown couch and a big armchair with a knitted blanket over it. I go through an archway into the kitchen. There's our old wooden table, the one we had in the last apartment. Now it has three metal chairs with red plastic seats. I go back to the living room and look over at the stairs behind the couch.

"Go on up, honey," Mom says. "Your room is on the left."

Our half of the upstairs has two bedrooms and a bathroom. Mom's right. This is the most room we've ever had.

I've never had a bedroom of my own before. I open the door on the left. The room is long and narrow, and there's a window at the end. The bedspread is pink like the curtains. It feels soft. I sniff.

Everything smells new. I guess Mom and Les just bought these things. There's a wooden dresser, and on top there's a mirror in a big curly wooden frame. I open the top drawer, and it's empty. I think about the rusty pink locker. From the window, I see a little yard and a garage. Les's car is in the driveway.

On most nights, like before when I lived alone with Mom, I lie in bed and wait. In the dark, it feels like something is going to happen. I don't know what, but it scares me. Sometimes I even wake up in the middle of the night with my heart pounding. I slip way down under the covers. After a while, if nothing happens, I go back to sleep.

In the morning, sometimes I look out my window and watch Les walk to the garage. Some days he doesn't wear his hat, and I can see skin through his hair. He walks slowly. He's tall, and his shoulders are big. Mom says he works at a factory called IBM. He's been there most of his life.

Right away, I start at a new school. Mom takes me over, and they put me in the seventh grade. The school seems okay, but I try to stay by myself. I don't know how long I'll be here.

By the time spring comes, Mom is carrying her jelly glass around. And it has a dark brown drink in it, just like before. I guess she goes out to the store for her stuff while I'm at school and Les is at work. One time when I get home, I find her staring in the mirror in the hallway and crying. That night, like lots of nights, she and Les talk real loud in their bedroom. I keep my door closed. I don't want to hear what they're saying.

Some days, when Mom's really upset, I think about the time the ambulance took her away and the ladies put me in the Home.

But if those ladies come again, Mom could get sent back to the hospital. I try not to think about that part. I just go upstairs to stay out of her way.

One nice day when it's warm outside, I hurry home carrying my books. It's almost the end of the school year, and I need to study for exams. I stop in the kitchen for a glass of apple juice. Mom is sitting at the table. She's squeezing that jelly glass really tight. Her hair is messed up. She's shaking her head and words come out but I can't understand them. I put my glass of juice on the counter and lean down close to her face to hear her better. Right away, she jerks her arm up and her drink goes all over the floor. Both of us look down. There's a big brown wet spot spreading across the linoleum.

"Damn it, Sue," Mom yells. She stands up and her eyes look cold and hard. "For God's sake, can't you do anything right?"

She starts across the room toward the cupboard. The glass is in her hand. She's going after her bottle. I look at the floor. The wet part looks brownish gray and dirty. I better fix this in a hurry.

I pull the metal bucket out from under the sink and run some water in it. Then I grab the old mop from the broom closet and start pushing it around on the wet spot. By now, Mom is back at the table. I can feel her watching me.

"You're making more of a mess." Her voice is loud, angry. I feel sick in my stomach. Pretty soon, like the other times, she'll yell at me for being "just like your father."

I keep trying to clean up the brownish mess on the floor. When I lean down to wring out the mop, she smacks me hard on my back. I jump away and almost knock over the pail. Mom stands up and her chair turns over. I back up a little. She's holding her glass up like it's a special toast or something. But her eyes look like a dark storm.

As I watch, she turns the glass over and pours her drink on the floor where I just mopped.

"Now clean it again," she tells me, her voice loud, hard. "And this time, do it right." With her free hand she grabs my hair.

My hand flies out and slaps her on the arm. I step back right away.

Don't hit your mother! Don't. Don't.

We're yelling and crying. I'm so hurt, I don't know what I'm saying. We're fighting and slapping at each other when the back door opens and Les comes running in. He grabs Mom's arm and pulls her away. My throat hurts and I'm breathing hard. As he drags her up the stairs, she shouts, "Damn it, you have no right. She is *my* daughter." I hear her crying.

I lean over the kitchen sink. I keep swallowing so I won't throw up. After a while, I run cold water over the scratches and red marks on my arms and hands. I smooth some water over my face. When I stop crying, I slip into the front room and sit on the edge of the couch. The whole house is quiet. I think a lot about Mom and how hard it is to live here, but I don't know what to do.

Les's footsteps are heavy coming down the stairs. The living room is almost dark. He stops at the bottom and turns on the overhead light.

"I called the Home," he tells me as he walks across the room. "I asked them to come and get you." He turns to face me.

I look at his eyes. They're wet.

"It's not your fault, Sue. It's the way she is." He blows his nose on a red and white handkerchief that looks like a bandana. "I'm sorry about this."

We sit at opposite ends of the couch. My mind slows down, like it's sleeping. Finally there's a knock on the front door. Les gets up slowly and goes over to open it. I lean over so I can see around him. There's a woman wearing a fancy suit standing on the porch. She has a notebook and a pen in her hands. I've never seen her before. Les goes outside and they begin to talk. The front door swings part way closed. I stand up and tiptoe across the room until I'm close to the half-open door. I want to hear what they're saying.

"I think you should take her back," Les says. "It's not good for her here." I see the woman nod. She's got her notebook open and is writing things down.

"How bad is it?" she asks.

They put their heads close together and talk some more, but I can't hear.

Then the lady steps back, straightens her jacket and her voice rises. "If I take her now, when can you bring her things, Mr. Whalen?"

I lean into the doorway, and the woman sees me. Her eyes are dark and serious. She looks at me, then glances at her watch.

"Come outside, Sue," she says. "It's time to get going."

I turn back and look at the old radio sitting there in the dark. I take a deep breath. I walk by Les and touch him on the arm, as if to say "it's okay," or something. I don't really know.

BACK AT THE HOME

Cottage No. 3

Not long after I moved back into Orton, Miss Hartford called us all downstairs. She passed around a list of who is going to live in each of the new cottages. I got assigned to Cottage No. 3. I grabbed Donna's hand and squeezed it when we learned we'd be in the same house. I looked at the list again. It showed Miss Hartford going to Cottage No. 2. That meant we were going to have a new housemother.

It's the end of August now, almost time for school to start. Boy, does that make me feel safe! All of us girls have been hauling boxes and bags and pillows down to the new cottages for the past few weeks. My T-shirt is wet and sticky, and the blister on my heel just broke. I can hardly wait for this move to be over, and for school to begin. We're lugging the last of the big cartons into the new cottages when Miss Hartford shows up.

"All Cottage 3 girls, it's time to line up in the hallway." She waits for us to sort ourselves out. When we're in a raggedy line, she announces, "You're going to meet your new housemother. She's moving in today."

I look around. We're all hot and sweaty and dirty.

"Shouldn't we clean up?" I ask. The rest of the Cottage 3 girls snort and laugh.

"Never mind, Sue," Miss Hartford answers. "We don't have time."

I rub my dirty hands on my shorts in case the new one wants to shake hands.

"Girls, this is Mrs. Labee. She'll be your housemother."

She's short, especially next to Miss Hartford. She's even shorter than me, and I'm only five-foot-four. Her hair is bright red and kind of frizzy. She looks like she's already annoyed or upset about something.

"Nice to meet you girls. I hope we'll all get along just fine."

Everybody stares. Oh boy.

In a few minutes, we're all back at work. Mrs. Labee and Miss Hartford disappear into the place where the housemother will live. It's kind of an apartment that's mostly on the main floor. There's also a door at the end of the hall upstairs. I guess that's so the housemother can get to our bedrooms fast if we're noisy or making trouble after lights-out.

I lug the last box of my clothes upstairs to my room and sit down on the edge of a mattress. Two of the bedrooms are big and have four beds. My room only has two. Donna and her sister Ellen have the other small room. It's down the hall. Since I don't have a roommate yet, this feels like a pretty safe place, at least for now.

After we've been in the cottage a few weeks, I can tell some of the girls are talking to Mrs. Labee about me. It's the ones who don't like me. I bet it's Nan, for sure. The back of her hair is ragged where she chopped it off last week. Right before she cut it, I heard her yelling, "Nobody can tell me what to do with my hair."

Nan and the others must have told Mrs. Labee they called me Goody-Goody because now sometimes she calls me that. It's like she wants to be one of them.

"Here's another box that belongs upstairs, Miss Goody-Goody," Mrs. Labee says. She points to a big box with the bottom falling out.

"My name is Sue," I say in a pretty loud voice, but she just turns her back on me. Nan laughs. She sounds so tough it's scary. Today she's got on boy's pants, or maybe they're men's. When she leans over, the tan cotton gets so tight around her legs she looks like those guys in the magazines who lift weights.

One time Mrs. Labee stops me in the hallway, my hands full of a couple books for school. She takes hold of my arm and calls to the other girls. "Look at Sue. She works *much* too hard." The girls giggle.

I'm sure glad Donna is in my cottage.

The cottage is a lot bigger than that duplex where Mom and Les live. This has three floors. You come in on the middle floor where there's a big living room with lots of windows. I looked in here when I was wandering around last winter. That's when I saw the fireplace. Yesterday I heard Mrs. Labee tell one of the girls we're going to get a TV soon. That would be cool. I saw one downtown in a store window.

Every time I come in the front door, I go through a little room that has a sink and a row of cubbyholes where we hang our coats.

Mrs. Labee calls it the mud room. In the corner, there's a big gray hair dryer. It's the kind they show in beauty parlor pictures in magazines. To me it looks like a metal beehive.

There's even a phone for us to use. It's on a long shelf in the hall that runs next to the mud room, but there's no place to sit. You have to stand up when you're talking. Right away, Mrs. Labee put a kitchen timer with big numbers next to the phone. When you make a call, she sets it for three minutes. When I call Mom, I don't even talk that long.

On the bottom floor, there's a long dining room and a kitchen. If you walk through the dining room, you come out in the rec room. It has a ping pong table. All the floors down here are hard and red. They feel like the sidewalks outside. Donna says they're made of concrete.

We eat in the cottage now, but we don't really cook anything. For breakfast, one of the older girls puts bowls and cereal and milk on the table and makes toast for us. Lunch and supper come down from the Main Building on a big metal cart with wheels. Last week we got ravioli, white bread, and canned green beans three times. So far, the food is really yucky and nobody says grace. I miss seeing Mac in the dining room.

Mostly I stay by myself, unless I'm hanging out with Donna. Some afternoons I wander over to the edge of Home property. We're allowed to go that far without a signed pass. I like to sit in the shade of the big maple tree and watch the people who live in regular houses on Home Avenue. Some of them drink soda pop while they sit on their porches. Sometimes an older man three houses away hauls a big red lawnmower out of the garage and cuts the grass. I can almost smell it from here.

Other times I wander down to the Home's vegetable garden. I like to sit in the sun and eat warm tomatoes. It's so far away from the cottages, I can sing out loud and nobody hears me. I know all the words to "Oh Susannah" and "Blue Moon." I think about Mom and how we used to sing together. It's been a few months since Mom and I got into that fight. I wonder if she thinks about it.

One night, not long after we moved into the cottages, a Home boy named Stewart ran away and stole a big old furniture truck. He crashed it on the bridge over the river. The next day when a bunch of us went down to the Susquehanna River during swim time, we saw the front part of the truck wrapped around the bridge. I guess Stewart got through it okay, but he's not here anymore. He was sure cute. He had curly black hair and blue eyes. He was our only orphan. I bet he got sent to reform school.

Nan

School's started! Yippee! I turned thirteen this summer and I'm in the eighth grade, and we've been in the cottages a while now and no new girl has shown up to be my roommate. Cool! I love having my own room. I don't tell Mrs. Labee though. She'd just grab a trouble-maker from another room and put her in here to try and upset me. Most of the tough girls like our new housemother. She makes them laugh. I wish she'd leave. So does Donna.

I'm in my room getting ready for bed. Tonight I put on my oldest pajamas. The worn-out fabric is so soft, and it just makes me feel good. The cuffs are raggedy but that's okay.

Before lights-out, I turn on the lamp that's on the table next to my bed. It has a little metal shade shaped like a paper cup. The circle of light it makes is so small, you can't see it from the hallway. I pull

The Catcher in the Rye out from under my bed. It's such a cool story, but I don't think the librarian likes me reading it.

"Lights-out!" Mrs. Labee hollers from the far end of the hall. She always stays right by her apartment when she does this. "Good night, girls." I hear her door close.

I turn off the bright overhead light. Then I climb in bed and get settled with my book. When I tilt the blue metal shade a little, there's just enough light to see the page.

I read until my eyes start to close. I turn down the edge of the page, even though the librarian told us not to, and reach for the little on-off button on the metal base of my lamp. I'm so sleepy that I don't even put the book back under the bed. I just tuck it under my pillow, turn on my side, and close my eyes.

Suddenly, hands are pressing my face, my shoulders, my chest. My eyes fly open. Someone's in my bed, someone's shoving themselves up against me from behind. I strike out with one arm, and it's slapped down. I try to curl up tight in a ball.

I smell hair, soap, cigarettes. Hands grab for my breasts, then slide between my legs. "Shh," I hear. "Just relax. You'll like this, honey." It's Nan. She's breathing on the back of my neck, and her mouth is in my hair. I try hard to get away, but she holds on.

She throws one leg across me to pin me down. It's like a chest of drawers fell on me. Her front is against my back, her arms around me, her hands moving up and down, her hair and face pushing into my neck.

"Get off me," I yell. She doesn't stop.

"Shut up. You want Labee in here, Goody?" Her voice is rough.

"Leave me alone!"

I pull my body in tight, like I'm getting ready to run. Nan's hands push up under my pajama top.

The lamp. I need to hit her with the lamp. It's behind her. I turn over, slapping at her, hitting her face. Her arms get tighter trying to hold me still.

I knee her. She folds down a bit, just enough to give me some room.

"Stop it, bitch," she mutters. She's breathing hard now.

I grab the lamp. The cord comes flying out of the wall. I smack her in the face with the metal shade. It comes loose, but I don't stop. I hit her with it again, and drag myself out of the bed.

"Get out of here," I tell her, my voice hard. "Stay away from me."

She's standing on one side of the bed. I'm standing on the other. The lamp is still in my hand. My body is shaking.

Finally Nan turns and starts toward the door. I watch her in the pale moonlight coming in through the window.

"I'll get you later, bitch," she says in a raspy, low voice.

I'm breathing fast, holding the lamp, waiting.

She opens the door and leaves, pulling it closed behind her.

After Nan goes, I stay awake for what feels like hours. When I stop shaking, I straighten out the shade as best I can, and I keep my tiny light on, just in case. But she doesn't come back. When morning comes, I drag myself out of bed. I feel even more tired than when I got back in bed last night.

I think a lot before I go down to breakfast. What if she told the other girls? What if Mrs. Labee knows? Would they think what she did is okay?

I pull on my jeans and a heavy brown sweater. The more I'm covered up, the better. The bathroom is empty. I splash water on my face, pat it dry, and stop to look at myself in the big mirror that's over the sink. Did I make this happen? Hell no, I tell myself. She's just off her rocker. I heard about girls like her, but I never got attacked by one. It makes my cheeks flame with anger just to think about her.

They're all at breakfast when I get downstairs. Nan's sitting at the far end of the table by Mrs. Labee. I sit down at the other end. I don't look around. I concentrate on putting cereal in the bowl in front of me and pouring milk on my cereal.

"Want some toast?" It's Ellen, Donna's sister. She's holding the blue and white plate with pieces of bread out to me. I shake my head, but I take the plate and pass it along.

The girls up by Mrs. Labee are talking and laughing about a Glee Club concert that's going to happen at the high school today. I'm the only one here who's still at the junior high. Right now I'm really thankful about that. I don't have to think about running into Nan walking the halls at school.

After we eat, just before we get up from the table, I take a quick look over at Nan. Her cheek has a cut on it and there's still some little spots of blood around it. She turns. It's almost as if she knows I'm looking at her. She smiles. It's a bad kind of smile, one that tells me she's pissed and will get back at me later.

I carry my cereal bowl from the dining room through the doorway to the kitchen and set it beside the others on the counter. Donna comes up next to me.

"Are you feeling okay?" she asks.

"Shhh," I whisper. "I'll tell you later."

"Okay," she whispers back. She gives my arm a quick squeeze and takes off. I stand at the sink, my back to the kitchen.

"Good morning, Goody."

It's her, it's that voice. I don't answer.

"Sorry if I woke you last night. Just came to borrow your book, you know?" She stops and waits. I turn and look at her, stare at her face. I don't move an inch.

"Didn't mean to bother you, Goody. We'll get together another time." Her eyes are like slits and she's smiling.

Girls are all over the kitchen, dropping off plates and cups, tossing out paper napkins, putting milk back in the fridge. Nan and I are frozen by the sink. I straighten up and make myself almost as tall as she is. She must be fifty pounds heavier. Her arms pop out of her white T-shirt like a body-builder. I stand in front of her and look her in the eye. Then slowly, she steps aside to let me pass. I keep my eyes straight ahead and walk by her as though she means nothing to me. My heart is going a million beats a minute, but I keep moving like I know what I'm doing.

Later on, Donna and I are in the mud room putting on our coats and scarves to go to our different schools.

"Did she hurt you?" she asks, keeping her voice quiet. Her eyes are so clear and good, so strong. Somehow she knows.

I shake my head.

"Are you okay?"

I lean close to her ear.

"See the scratch on her face?"

Donna nods. She's excited now.

"She came after me last night. In a weird way. Like we were boyfriend and girlfriend, you know?"

Donna nods again and looks down.

"I hit her with my lamp. And if she tries it again, I swear I'll rip her eyes out."

The utility closet

"Sue, where are you?"

It's Mrs. Labee. She sounds mad, as usual.

I put my eighth-grade Social Studies book on my bed and come out of my room. When I look down the stairs, I see her standing on the landing, where the staircase turns. A whole bunch of girls are behind her giggling.

"I have a job for you, young lady." She points down toward the dining room. "Get down there. Now."

"But I'm doing my—"

"NOW, I said!" I hear Nan laughing.

I start down the stairs, making sure not to touch anyone as I pass. When I get to the bottom floor, I look back up at the landing. Everybody is still gathered around Mrs. Labee.

"Do you know where the utility closet is?"

"Yes, Mrs. Labee." Of course I know.

The girls laugh some more.

"Go inside the closet and close the door." She stares at me. I stare back. Why is she doing this?

The closet is right across from the stairs. I don't know what I'm in for, but it won't be good. I take a deep breath and go inside and pull the door shut behind me.

Right away, I reach up and yank the light chain. The bulb goes on. The room is so small, there's barely space enough to turn around. In front of me is the big white sink. It's deep enough to hold the mop bucket. I take a step back and bump into the shelves that are full of soap and brushes and steel wool. I stare at the sink.

The last time Mrs. Labee came after me, it was in the middle of the night. I woke up to find her shaking me.

"I have a job for you," she told me, right there in my pitch black room hours after lights-out.

"Is something wrong?" I asked her.

No answer. She just grabbed me by the arm and pulled me out of my bed and down the stairs. She didn't even turn on the hall lights. We ended up in the rec room.

"Get on your hands and knees and scrub the wax off this floor." Her voice was flat, mean. She was wearing a bright green robe, the kind that looks like bath towels. And she had her pointy-toed shoes on.

"Use really hot water and steel wool," she told me. "Do it right. Or else. I'll be back to check."

I spent the whole night lugging pail after pail of hot water from the utility closet. I scrubbed for a long time, waiting for her. Finally the sun began to come through the window. She never came back. In fact, she never even mentioned this to me again.

"How's the utility closet?" Mrs. Labee asks. "Are you cozy in there?"

I don't answer.

"Turn on the water." Silence. "Only the hot water. It needs to get *really* hot. Do you understand me?"

My heart pumps right behind my eyes. My head hurts. I don't know what else to do. I turn the water on.

It doesn't take long for steam to begin to fill the tiny room. It climbs up the sides of the sink, then up the walls. I stick my finger under the water and yank it back. It's so hot, it burns me. I wipe sweat out of my eyes.

There are dark wet spots on the wall. My shirt is sticking to my skin. The hot water runs and runs. When I start coughing, I turn my face away from the door so she won't hear me.

"Is the water hot yet?" She's yelling now.

I don't answer her. I hate her. I turn away from the sink, rest my forehead on the edge of one of the shelves and close my eyes. The water runs on and on and on.

If I try to get out, she'll get me sent to a really bad foster home and I'll get beat up all the time. It will be even worse than this.

"Sue? Can you hear me?"

Don't answer. Don't give her that satisfaction.

"You can come out now."

I turn the water off. In the silence, I pick a rag off a shelf to wipe the sweat off my face. I pull myself together.

As soon as I open the door, steam comes pouring out around me. Girls are crowded by the door. Someone is laughing real loud. Probably Nan. My hair sticks to my head. My back and arms are soaked. It's like I've been boiled alive.

Mrs. Labee is standing right in front of me, her arms folded, her eyes cold. Now all the girls are screeching with laughter and Nan is jumping up and down, slapping her hand against the wall. I lift my head and walk past them going straight up the stairs. My skin is red and hot and tight but my back is straight. I go in my room and close the door behind me. As soon as I'm alone, I stuff my fist in my mouth. I refuse to let any of them hear me cry.

Runaways

I'm on my knees in the mud room, which is not how I want to spend Saturday. Every week, Mrs. Labee makes me push a scrub brush around on this hard tile floor. She told me I can't use a mop. "Knowing you, you'd do a sloppy job," she said. "On your knees, and that's final." It's my least favorite job and she knows it. That's why she makes me do it.

I'm pushing my way around the floor when I hear two girls talking in the living room next door.

"Let's get the hell out of here," one of them says. "And I mean, we do it tonight."

"Yeah. Let's do it!"

Get the hell out of here? I lift my head and stop scrubbing. I bet it's Nan talking to that new girl. I think her name is Karen.

"But what if we get caught?"

Yup, that's the new girl. She has long dark oily-looking hair, and she has a sneer on her face most of the time. As soon as she dragged her boxes of stuff into the cottage, she and Nan hit it off.

"Shit. Who cares?"

That's Nan for sure. She swears a lot.

I wipe my hands on my jeans and stand up. I move slow so they won't hear me. If I can find out what kind of bad stuff is about to happen, maybe I can stay out of their way.

"Come on," Nan says to Karen. "Are you chicken or what?" Nan's making trouble. So what's new.

I slide closer to the mud room door so I can watch them through the narrow opening between the door and the wall. They've pulled two brown plastic chairs close together, the kind that are scattered around the living room.

I turn my head a little to look at Karen. Even sitting down, she's tall and skinny. She has on a long black shirt that hangs on her. Her bones stick out around the collar.

When I lean forward to hear better, the door shifts making a soft creaking sound. Nan sits up straight and turns toward the mud room. She looks like a hunting dog that just smelled a fox. I freeze.

"Hey Goody. You in there?" She pauses. "It's Saturday. I bet that's you scrubbing the floor in there."

My mind starts going in crazy circles. How do I get out of this?

"Get out here, Goody." Now her voice is heavy, dark.

I stand up, open the door, and step into the doorway.

Nan stares deep into my eyes. I don't turn away. "You heard us, right?"

I get a picture in my mind of the time Nan stuck her leg out and tripped a girl on the stairs. The girl crashed on the landing and her arm twisted under her so bad she couldn't get up. Nan laughed and stepped right over her.

I don't answer.

She's got that grin on her face, the kind she gets when she's about to cause pain. She snaps her fingers. "That's it, Goody. We'll go out your window."

"Hey," says oily-haired Karen. She looks at me. "You're the only one with no roommate, so nobody else will wake up. How about it, Goody?" She crosses her long, skinny legs and stares at me as she cracks her knuckles. She does that a lot.

"Yeah, let's use her window." Nan points at me. "It's close to the ground. What do you say, Goody?"

"I guess so." My voice is quiet.

"What was that, Goody?" She wants to hear it again.

"I said okay." This time I'm louder. I don't care if she uses my window to run away from this cottage. I just want her to leave me the hell alone.

Nan pulls herself up and does a slow walk past me. She smells like cigarettes, as always. She takes the stairs two at a time, her legs pounding their way to the top. Tall Karen slinks by me and sneers at me. I quick squat down and start pushing the scrub brush around on the tile. I hear Karen whisper, "See you after lights-out, Goody."

After supper, I climb the stairs up to my bedroom and close the door. The clock says it's not even 8. Lights-out is at 10.

I grab one of my new books from school and lie down on my bed. I stare at the same page for a long time. When the big round clock on the wall says it's almost 10, I get up and turn off the ceiling light. They'll come when the hallway and the rooms are dark. I cross back to sit on my bed and wait. I don't turn on the little lamp. The moonlight from the window touches the door.

I'm almost asleep when I hear the door open. I sit up straight really fast. Nan stops in the doorway. In the dim light from the moon, she looks around. As soon as she sees me sitting on the edge of the bed, she steps inside. Karen slips in behind her and slides the door closed. I stay where I am. I don't want any part of this.

Nan heads for the window with Karen right behind her. I wipe my palms on my jeans and make a kind of wish in my head. Maybe, just maybe, I won't get blamed for helping them run away.

Nan slides the window open and jiggles the screen until it pops out. She gets it loose so fast, I figure she's done this before. I hear a scraping sound as she sets the screen on the floor and leans the edge against the wall. Right away, she plunks her butt on the windowsill, pulls her legs up and drops over the ledge. Before I can blink, she's gone. I wince at the sound as she scrapes against the house on her way down. Good-bye Nan.

Now there's only the new girl and me.

I stand up.

Karen starts toward me. The moonlight shows her back is straight, like she's in charge now.

"You wanna come, Goody?" she whispers. Her eyes look wild and dark, like she's on something.

"No way," I tell her.

Karen goes back to the window and swings her tall body over the sill, disappearing into the night.

I watch and listen near the window. Nothing is moving out there. Nothing is happening in the hallway outside my room either. Maybe nobody knows Nan and Karen are gone.

I pull off my jeans and shirt and stuff them into my laundry bag in the closet. I get into my pajamas and sit back down on the edge of my bed.

The window's still open. I'm so cold and tired, it's hard to know if my head makes sense. What if they come back? I leave the screen leaning against my bedroom wall, just in case. I curl up on my side and pull my knees up to my chest. I lie like this, waiting in the cold night air until a little bit of sun starts to show in the window. Okay, I figure, they're not coming back. At least not through my window. I manage to wiggle the screen back in place and slide the window closed. By the time I pull the warm blanket up under my chin, my eyes are closed. I press my icy cold hands between my thighs for warmth. I'm almost too tired to be nervous.

The next afternoon after school, I see Mrs. Labee talking on the phone in the hall. "Where are they now?" she asks. I duck into the mud room to listen.

"Uh huh. Well, bring them back." A pause. "Yes. To Mr. McPherson's office. We'll take it from there." She bangs down the receiver.

In the late afternoon, I see a police car drive slowly past our cottage. It stops in front of the Main Building. A policeman gets out, yanks open the back door, and stands beside the car. Nan and Karen climb out of the back seat. There's brown stuff that looks like mud all over the back of Nan's shirt and pants.

After dinner, Mac marches them down to the cottage and into Mrs. Labee's apartment. In about an hour, he leaves looking angry. The girls stay in there for a long time. Maybe they'll tell Mrs. Labee how they used my window to get out of the house. Boy, I hope not.

Alone in my room, I hear sounds coming from the hallway. I quick get out of bed and press my ear against my door. I hear doors opening and closing. Then silence. They must be in their rooms by now. And Mrs. Labee's not coming after me. At least not right now.

I creep back to my bed, pull up the blankets, and stare into the darkness until I fall asleep.

Think about it

So much is going on, it makes my head spin. I grab a jacket in the mud room and start up toward the Main Building. Pretty soon, I stop. What if I see Mac, and he asks me how things are going? Geez, if he finds out how Nan and Mrs. Labee treat me, he might go after them. Then I don't know *what* they'd do to me.

I turn around and walk down through the garden toward the river. I pull on my jacket. The wind is making the October leaves fly around. When I get close to the river, I find a big log that will block the wind and I sit behind it. I pull my knees up and wrap my arms around them.

You need to think about this, I tell myself. My eyes start to tear up, and I rub them on the arm of my jacket. Don't cry now, silly, just sit here and figure out what you're going to do.

Nothing. That's the first thing I think. How can I do anything? Not unless I'm willing to tell someone what's going on. Who could I tell? Mac. He's the only one. He might move me to another cottage, but that doesn't mean Nan and the other girls who don't like me wouldn't come find me. And who knows what Mrs. Labee would do. Geez, I wouldn't be safe in another house either.

I pull my jacket collar up to keep the wind off. I think about what I've done to get through stuff. I fought back when Nan came after me. And I didn't fold after Mrs. Labee tried to boil me in the utility closet. And I have Donna as my best friend. And Ellen likes me, too; at least, she doesn't hurt me.

Maybe they'll send Nan to reform school since she ran away. Just imagining her being gone lets my shoulders drop down to normal and my breathing work okay. Hey, they sent Stewart up when he ran away and stole that truck, right? And Helen, when she started that fire and pushed Miss Hartford down the stairs. Geez, I wish they knew how bad Nan is to me. But I don't dare tell. She'd beat the crap out of me if she found out. And I don't know what Mrs. Labee would do.

The wind blows harder. I pull my jacket tight around me and stick my hands in my pockets. I watch the big wooden float bob around out in the river. It's like there's a dock in the middle of the water. It was fun swimming out to that float last summer. And, when I think about it, some of the new girls in Miss Hartford's cottage are okay. It was cool to swim with them and splash and laugh. They don't seem like they fight all the time. Plus, they're younger.

I stand up and brush the leaves and pieces of dried grass off my jeans. Think about Donna, I tell myself. And Ellen. And the other nice girls. Hang out with them. Don't let Nan and the others hurt you inside your head. Yeah, maybe they can smack you around a little, but they can't change the way you are, the way you think about stuff.

"Just be cool, Sue." I say this out loud. "You'll make it through."

I stick my hands in my pockets and walk fast back up to the cottage, kicking dry leaves.

Moving on

I didn't see anybody take her away, but she's nowhere around the cottage. Karen's still here, but I haven't seen Nan in days.

When it's quiet upstairs, I come out of my room. The hall is empty. I tiptoe to the room Nan shared with three other girls. I listen at the door. No sounds come from inside. I open the door a little and look in. Her bed is stripped. The closet door is part way open. One side is empty. Something inside me relaxes. She wasn't my only nightmare, but she was a big one. And now it looks like she's gone.

I knock on the door to the room that Donna and Ellen share. "Donna? Are you in there?"

"Yeah," she answers. "What's up? Come on in."

I go in and collapse on the foot of her bed. It's Saturday, and Donna is curled up, as usual, reading a magazine about fancy clothes and going on dates.

"Nan's gone," I tell her. Then I jump up and let out a big whoop, the kind you hear at football games. Donna laughs so hard, she starts to choke. I slap her on the back, and now we're both laughing and bouncing up and down on the edge of the bed.

"I don't know why she picked on you, Sue," Donna says, shaking her head. "You never did anything to her."

"Yeah. But I never gave in to her either. And she hated that."

I walk around a pile of shoes and a stack of magazines and look out the window.

"I need to get my report card signed," I tell Donna. "And I don't want to go to Mrs. Labee for this."

"Yeah. You have all A's?"

"One B," I tell her.

"Too good. She's sure to make fun of you." Then, after a minute, she says, "Hey! Take it to Mac. He's really in charge here, why not have him sign it?"

I look at her and we grin and slap hands.

"That is such a cool idea," I tell her. "I'll do it right now."

I wave on my way out of her room.

"See you later," she hollers.

"That's for sure," I yell back from halfway down the hall.

Laughing, I run into my room and grab the report card out of the top drawer of my dresser. I put on a sweater, stick the report card in my pocket, and run up to the Main Building.

His real name is John Francis McPherson, but we all call him Mac. When I saw him at the big table in the main dining room that first morning, I got a safe feeling. As he said grace, I felt he was talking to me, Sue Pickering, the new girl. It wasn't the words so much as the sound of his voice that told me, somehow, things would work out. Whenever I can, I stand near him.

As I hurry up the sidewalk to his office, I let myself believe just for one minute the Home may turn out to be okay.

I want to do the report card in private, so I sit on the steps outside the Main Building and wait for him to come out of his office. It's a warm red and yellow fall day so I don't mind. In just a few minutes, Mac comes whistling through the big doors of the Main Building.

"Hey," he says. He looks down, surprised to see me sitting there. "How's it going, Sue?" He gives me a smile. He almost always does that.

For a moment, I stare at the sidewalk. Should I tell him about how Mrs. Labee treats me? I don't think so. If he says anything to her, it would make more of a mess for me down at the cottage.

"It's going okay," I stand up and smile back.

"How's eighth grade? Do you like it?"

"Yeah. It's pretty cool." Now I have a big smile on my face.

He starts walking down the sidewalk. I hurry along beside him.

Soon, he stops and looks at me like he's figuring things out. He puts out his hand. "Got it?"

Somehow he knows I brought my report card. I slide it out of my pocket and hand it to him. He stops right where he is and opens it. Then he nods his head and starts to read out loud.

"Sue works hard." He looks over at me and nods.

"Sue is a good student." He grins.

"It's a pleasure having Sue in my class."

By now we've walked a ways down the slope toward the cottages. I hope he's not going to go with me all the way to Cottage 3. The idea of Mac and Mrs. Labee talking about my report card makes it hard to breathe. I unbutton my cardigan. Now it's too warm.

"Only one B. This is a lot better than just okay, young lady. This is very good." Then he asks, "What did the girls in your cottage have to say about your grades?"

Oh, wow. I look away. I wonder if he knows how bad they treat me.

"They don't know," I tell him.

"Has Mrs. Labee seen your card?"

My mouth drops open and my eyes get big, but all I say is, "No."

He nods. He's thinking. Then right there, while we're standing on the sidewalk, he pulls his ballpoint pen out of his jacket pocket and clicks it open.

"Turn around," he tells me. I feel the pen moving on my shoulder through my sweater as he signs my card. When he hands it back to me, he looks pretty serious. I pull my sweater around me.

"Sue, do you ever come up to the library?"

"What library?"

"Well, there's sort of a library in the Main Building. It's right next to my office. It's small, but we've got some good books." He frowns. By now we're walking again.

"Have you ever read *The Secret Garden*?"

I shake my head.

"I bet you'd like it."

We trudge along some more. It feels good to be walking side by side with Mac. And to find out about a library? Holy cow.

"You know, it's pretty quiet there. Hardly anyone ever comes in." He stops and turns to face me. "You know what?" His voice is strong and sure. "When you want to visit the library, you tell Mrs. Labee you're coming up to the Main Building, that's all. And, if she asks, tell her that I said it's okay. Got that?"

I nod. Mac pats me on the shoulder and takes off across campus. I continue on down toward the cottage, holding my signed report card tight in my hand. Somebody smart who cares about me thinks I'm doing a good job! And he doesn't even know I went to fourteen schools before I got to the seventh grade. I keep that list in the back of my sweater drawer.

Supper at Mac's house

I'm sweeping the sidewalk in front of the cottage, singing to myself. Nan's gone, and Karen ignores me, and I love my Social Studies class. I'm feeling pretty good when I see Mac walking up the sidewalk. He's whistling, and he's got his hands in his pockets. I like it when he whistles.

"Nice day, huh?" he calls to me.

"Yeah," I answer. I think about fall. "And it smells good, too."

He laughs. Then he turns and comes down our sidewalk.

"So, Sue." He's taking his time. I just stand and wait. "Jean and I were wondering if you'd like to come to our house for supper some night."

Come to their house for supper? I look at the bright blue sky, the red and yellow leaves, the pile of dead weeds on the sidewalk. I've never even been to Mac's house. I walk by it every day on my way to school. There's a front porch with white chairs and a small table. I know he has a wife named Jean, and Sally and Andy are his kids. I think they're close to my age, but we go to different schools.

I look up at him. "I'll ask Mrs. Labee," I tell him.

"That's great. Let her know we'll expect you at six o'clock this Friday. That sound okay?" I nod. "Any problems, you let me know."

That night, right before lights-out, I watch for Mrs. Labee. I think about how to say this.

Pretty soon, she's passing me on her way to her apartment. "Mrs. Labee?" She turns and stares at me. It's like she's always surprised to see me.

"Mac and Mrs. McPherson invited me to come to their house for supper." I look at her. Her eyes are cold, like always. I keep talking. "They want me to come on Friday." Nothing. Finally, I ask for permission. "Is that okay?"

She snorts and shakes her head. "Sure, go ahead, Goody. Nobody here will miss you." When she turns and disappears into her rooms, I thumb my nose at the air.

On Friday, I leave my school clothes on so I'll look okay for dinner. I even wear my brown shoes, the ones the man in the shoe store said were orthopedic. They look like an old lady's shoes, but I'm supposed to wear them.

When I walk up the porch steps, I see Mac through the front window. He's sitting on the couch reading the newspaper. I knock and wait. He opens the door.

"Sue, welcome."

"Hi."

I follow him into the living room. His kids are lying on the floor in front of the couch. Andy has a book open. Sally's looking at the funnies.

"Sally and Andy, this is Sue. She's in the eighth grade."

Sally plays with her sandy blond hair, twisting it around her finger. Andy stares at the ceiling.

"Hi," I say. I look down at my brown lace-up shoes.

"Hi," they answer.

Mac sits down on the couch. So do I.

There's a fireplace, and two chairs that match the couch I'm sitting on. All the furniture goes together. There's a big arch between the living room and the dining room. The table is already set. There are candles and a white tablecloth.

Mrs. McPherson comes out of the kitchen into the dining room. She's wiping her hands on her apron.

Mac calls to her. "Jean, this is Sue. I don't think you've met before."

She smiles and waves. I smile and wave back.

In a few minutes, she calls us in to supper. I try to stay behind the others. I want to see where I'm supposed to sit. Mac goes to one end of the table and pulls the chair out. Mrs. Mac sits down. Then he holds out another chair and motions to me. It's across from Sally and Andy. Mac sits at the other end of the table.

There's a big roast beef on a blue platter in front of him. I see piles of mashed potatoes and string beans in fancy blue bowls that have flowers painted on them. Everything matches. I fold my hands in my lap. Boy, this smells good, and it's all so pretty. Mom and I hardly ever had a meal like this. We don't get it like this in the cottages either, that's for sure.

Mac clears his throat and bows his head. Oh wow, I get to hear him say grace! I bow my head.

"Dear God, we thank you for this food and for Jean's care in preparing it. And bless our children, Sally and Andy, and bless Sue, who is here tonight and who is in our keeping. Amen."

It feels good to hear him say grace again, like in the old dining room in the Main Building. He even mentioned my name.

He stands up and tucks the end of his tie inside his shirt. Then he begins to slice the roast. He works carefully, like he cares about Mrs. Mac's cooking. From where I'm sitting, the kitchen light is shining behind Mac. It makes his hair look like a halo.

I watch as Mac puts food on the plates and hands them to the others. When he's getting my plate ready, he asks, "How would you like your meat?" I say medium, because that's what Sally said.

Out of the corner of my eye, I watch Mrs. Mac. She has a drink in her hand. It's brown, like Mom's. I hear the rattle of the ice. Mrs. Mac talks and laughs and takes sips from her pretty glass.

I keep my eyes down, like I'm looking at the plates with the flowers on them. I feel tight inside. I try to laugh at Andy's jokes and listen to Sally's stories about school. I have a second helping of mashed potatoes. It's warm in the dining room and the food tastes really good.

I bet Mrs. Mac doesn't drink like Mom, but I don't want to watch her anyway.

Zipper

"The best ones will be gone. We've gotta hurry!" It's the afternoon of Halloween and Donna is pulling me out the front door of the cottage. Somebody gave the Home a bunch of fancy dresses and Mrs. Labee told us we could pick one to wear to the party tonight.

"Okay, but where are they?"

"In the Main Building. Up in the storage room. Come on, slowpoke, before she changes her mind!" Donna grabs my arm and we run.

By the time we get there, the room is full of girls laughing, yelling, and pawing through two long racks of dresses. We push our way through.

"Who gave us these?" I holler to Donna.

"Don't know, don't care," she hollers back.

Pretty soon she grabs a long dress off the rack. It's purple, and it has a full skirt and floppy pink roses at the waist. "I want this one," she tells me. There's no place to change so she puts the gown on over her head and smoothes it down over her jeans.

I quick turn back to the rack. Pretty soon, I pull out a shiny, blue-green dress. It has long sleeves and a fancy neck. I saw one like it in a movie once.

I push my way through the crowd until I find Donna and give her a nudge. "Is this taffeta?" I'm holding the dress up so she can see it. She shrugs her shoulders, makes an I-don't-know face, and goes back to fussing with her purple gown. "Well, darn, Donna, are there any shoes in here?" I try to see around the mob of girls.

"Sue, you ask too many questions," Donna yells as she rolls her eyes.

I hurry and pull the gown on over my jeans. I look around but there's not even a mirror in here! I push my way back to Donna.

"Will this be okay?" I twirl around.

She takes a quick look. "It'll be great."

By now, Donna already has her purple gown off and is holding it close so no one can take it. "Let's get out of here," she calls out. I nod, and off we go, dresses hanging over our arms.

After supper that night, all the girls in the cottage race upstairs to get ready. I pull on my silky blue-green dress and stare at myself in the bedroom mirror. Something's wrong. I hike the skirt up so I won't trip and hurry down the stairs to the living room.

"Donna, what do I do? It's too big without my jeans." I turn around to show her.

"No wonder it's big, silly. You're not zipped up."

She points to a long metal zipper that goes up the side of my dress. I try to pull it. It's stuck. Donna is eager to leave for the party so I pull harder. The darn zipper is not moving.

"Hurry up, Sue. Don't make us be late." By now she's almost out the door.

I take a deep breath and yank it really hard. Then zap, it pinches my side so bad, it feels like somebody stuck me with a knife. I hold my breath and pull to get the zipper back down. I do this a lot. It won't move, and the zipper feels slippery. By now my fingers are wet and sticky. And they're red.

I hold my fingers up to show Donna, who's practically dancing in the doorway. "Donna, look. I'm bleeding." My voice is shaky.

She hurries over and stares at the bright red blood. Then she shifts my dress a little so she can see my side.

"Oh, wow, Sue. Geez, I better get Mrs. Labee. You wait here." She runs down the hall.

I don't move. I'm still standing in the living room, frozen, when Mrs. Labee comes hurrying in. Her eyes are hard and she has a big frown.

"Turn around so I can see what you've done." Boy, she sounds angry. Donna stands behind her staring at the floor.

As soon as I move, it feels like my side is on fire. My face scrunches up. I bite my lip hard so I won't cry. Mrs. Labee is glaring at my side.

"Honestly, Sue. How do you get yourself in such messes?" She shakes her head. "Well, go straight to the infirmary. And Donna, you'd better go along and make sure she gets there." She looks annoyed. "You got blood all over that dress, young lady. You'll pay for this."

It's dark out by now. Donna and I walk so slow, I can hear my dress scraping the ground. The zipper bites into me.

"Oh, wow, it hurts so much when I move."

"Shhh. Stop crying."

I take another step. Tears run down my cheeks and drip off my chin. Donna holds tight to my arm. We go like this the whole way. It takes us a long time to get to the infirmary.

The nurse helps me lie down on a cold metal table. I bite my lip again. I sure don't want to cry anymore. Donna watches from a chair in the corner.

The nurse turns me on my good side so she can see the cut. Each time she moves me, the hurt gets bigger. She carefully lifts my arm and stares. When she wiggles the zipper, I yell and pull away. I can't stop the tears this time.

"You need to lie very still while I do this, Sue." Her voice is firm, and she's frowning. "I'm afraid I'm going to have to cut your party dress apart to get this zipper out."

Soon it's so quiet, I can hear the nurse breathing. I try not to jump every time the cold scissors touch my skin. I feel her peel the dress back. She makes odd clicking noises with her mouth like things aren't right. When she pinches my skin together and wiggles the zipper again, I yell some more.

Donna makes a face and turns away.

"I'm sorry, Sue," the nurse says. She keeps her voice quiet. "This is really stuck."

She works for a long time. I bite my lip hard and try not to move.

"Finally," she announces and stops pulling.

She comes around the table until her white uniform is right in front of me. There are red spots all over it. I look up. She's holding the zipper in her hand. There's a lot of blood on it. She looks pale.

"No Halloween party for you, young lady. You'll be staying here tonight. We need to get that cut cleaned up, and I'll have to check it in the morning for any infection."

She smears on some medicine that stings. Then she puts a sticky bandage on me. She helps me sit up so I can peel off what's left of my ruined dress and get into one of the infirmary's nighties. It's open down the back and that feels weird.

"We're certainly done with *this*," she announces, dropping the zipper and the dress in a garbage pail. She turns to Donna. "You better go now or you're going to miss the party."

When the nurse leaves the room, Donna comes over and squeezes my hand. She looks so sad. "I'll come by for sure in the morning. And I'll bring you some Halloween candy."

I watch her go swishing out the door in her pretty purple dress.

My side is throbbing. It hurts a lot, like it's on fire. I shift a little so I can see my cut in the night-light beside my bed. Slowly I pull up the edge of my nightie. There's a big white bandage and smears of orange stuff on my skin. And my blue-green dress is ruined and I missed the party.

I close my eyes. Will things ever go right?

Payback

It's almost Thanksgiving when I find out the girl who's been my roommate for about a week is leaving. She stays so far away from me, I only know her first name. It's Venetia. One day, I get home from school and find her throwing her clothes into a cardboard box.

"What's up?" I ask her.

"I'm *outta* here." For once, her voice is loud, excited.

"Where to?"

"They got me into a foster home. It's on a farm. Isn't that cool?"

"Oh, great," I tell her, but I don't really mean it.

I make a quick trip to the bathroom. Some kids who were sent to foster homes came back all broken up and disappointed. They told stories about being made to work on farms until after dark and not getting enough food and stuff. Some even got beat up. I don't want to tell her about this. Anyway by the time I get back to our room, Venetia's gone.

Right away, I sit on my bed and think about Sharon. Her room is just down the hall. That girl started beating me up as soon as Nan left. It's like she took over. One night, a little while before Venetia moved in, Sharon sneaked in my room after lights-out and punched me and pinched my arms hard. When she finally left, she was laughing. I had bruises on my sides and my arms for a long time.

Now that I don't have a roommate, I bet Sharon will be after me again. I rub my sweaty palms on my jeans. Be careful, Sue, I tell myself.

After supper, I finish my homework and get my books ready for school tomorrow. Then I go down to the rec room. I sit by myself on one of the folding metal chairs they keep downstairs and watch two girls play ping pong. That's when I see Sharon. She's standing in the shadows on the other side of the rec room staring at me. She has pale eyes, like ice. Mom would say she's "mousey" looking. She's thin, but she hits really hard.

After lights-out, I watch Mrs. Labee go into her apartment and close the door. She doesn't care about stuff like this. She says we should "settle our own differences." I get tired just thinking about it.

That night I lie in bed waiting, keeping my little reading light turned on. It's not long before the door slides part way open.

There are three of them. Two stay by the door like they're standing guard. Sharon heads toward me grinning, raising her hands in fists. I climb out of bed fast. My heart is banging so hard, I can hardly breathe.

She smashes her fist into my side. Then she grabs my arm and pinches it hard over and over again. She does it up high where it won't show. I jerk away, but she grabs my hair and twists me around so I can't reach her.

I'm frozen. In my head, I float up to the ceiling. I hear Sharon muttering "bitch" over and over again every time she yanks my hair. Finally, she stops. By the time I turn around, she's gone.

As soon as the door closes behind them they start laughing in the hall. After a while, I turn off my reading light. The room is dark and quiet. My side is pounding and my arms hurt. Why does she do this to me? I brush the tears away. I hate this. Somehow, I have to make it stop.

All week long I wear shirts to cover my bruises. When Saturday comes, I'm on my knees scrubbing the floor in the mud room like always, and there's a knock on the hallway door. I don't get up. Everybody knows it's not locked. When I hear the knock again, I figure somebody needs help carrying something. I stand up, wipe my wet hands on my jeans, and reach for the doorknob.

It happens in slow motion, like a car wreck in the movies. I'm standing in the doorway when Sharon's fist comes straight for my face. I turn, and as my eyes close, her knuckles smash into my cheek. When I open my eyes, she's pulling her arm back again.

My heart's banging in my chest, and the world is now dark red.

I grab her by the hair and drag her over the threshold into the mud room. I'm breathing hard. I lean my back against the door to push it closed.

I haul her across the room, past the pail and scrub brush, past the bench where we take off our boots. I am heading for the big old gray metal hairdryer that stands in the corner.

Sharon grabs at my fingers, trying to pry them off her face, her hair. Her mouth is twisted, her eyes are slits. Somehow I get her up high enough so I can slam her head against the cold gray metal. I take a huge deep breath and do it over and over again.

"Bitch," she yells.

Slam.

"Stop it. I'll kill you!"

Slam.

Her voice is loud, fierce. She is dragging on my arm, yanking, tearing, anything to make me stop. My mind is wrecked. I hate her. I want to hurt her.

Girls scramble into the mud room and grab both of us.

"Stop it, Sue. Jesus. What the hell are you doing?" It's Donna. She's got her arms locked around me to hold me back.

Sharon is huddled on the floor under the hair dryer. Donna is staring at my hand. I look down. I am clutching a clump of Sharon's brown hair.

For the next week, I watch her. One of her eyes stays shut. Her face is covered with dark purple bruises that are turning yellow. She stays away from me.

I think about telling her I'm sorry, but that would be a lie.

"She liked to beat me up for no reason, and now look at what happened." I'm sitting with Donna on the bench in the mud room. We're staring at the bang marks on the hair drier. I feel confused.

Donna unbuttons the cuff of my long-sleeved plaid shirt and pushes up the sleeve. She points at what's left of the dark bruises, now a row of yellow and purple pinch marks on my arm.

"Don't forget where you got these," she says in a harsh whisper. "You can bet your life Sharon won't ever bother you again."

THINGS CHANGE

Good riddance

Donna hurries into my room and pulls the door shut behind her. I'm making my bed, folding and tucking the sheets into hospital corners like we're supposed to.

"What's up?" I ask her. When she doesn't answer, I stop working and look over at her. Her eyes are even bigger than usual, and she's bouncing up and down on her toes like she's nervous.

She leans toward me and whispers, "She's leaving."

"Who's leaving?" I hope she means Sharon. Maybe she's on her way out of the Home.

Donna pulls me over to the edge of the bed and sits me down.

"You're not gonna believe this," she tells me. "I heard Miss Hartford talking to Miss Rosa." She stops and looks in my eyes. She's serious about whatever this is.

"Will you just tell me what's going on?" I'm getting jumpy trying to figure this out.

"It's Mrs. Labee. She's going. We're not supposed to know yet."

"Oh my God. When?"

"It's gonna happen next week maybe. Anyway, soon. Miss Rosa will fill in for a while. I know she's sort of yucky, but she's better than Labee, that's for sure."

I stand up and take a deep breath. I need to get my mind to stop running around. I walk over to the window and stare out at the trees that are just beginning to show some leaves. I look at two girls going by on the sidewalk carrying a small box. I whisper to myself, "Mrs. Labee is leaving." I make a fast turn and face Donna.

"Are you sure?" I stare at her hard. I don't know what I'll do if this isn't real.

"Yeah, Sue," she says. "Geez, *Miss Hartford* said it. You know that means it's for real, right?"

I nod. "I guess so."

I sit down beside Donna.

"You know this means a lot to me, right?" My voice is low. I feel tears starting.

Donna reaches out and puts her arm across my shoulders.

"Everything's cool, Sue. It'll be over soon."

The next weekend, Mrs. Labee's boxes line the hallway outside the mud room. Miss Hartford and Miss Rosa gather us girls together to give her a good-bye party in the rec room. Somebody made a big cake that says, "Good luck Mrs. Labee" in bright pink letters. I bet Sharon did the letters. She's one of Labee's favorites.

I sit in the back of the room beside Donna and stare out the window. I don't look at Mrs. Labee. I don't say anything to her. When Ellen sticks a piece of cake under my nose, I turn away.

After about an hour, Miss Hartford announces, "It's time to say good-bye to Mrs. Labee, girls. Line up and get ready to give her a good-bye hug."

Donna squeezes my arm. She knows I'm not giving that woman a good-bye hug.

The line moves slowly. I'm way at the end. My mind whirls around trying to figure out what I'm going to do when I get up there. What do I say to this woman who was so mean, so cruel, so awful to me?

Miss Hartford is standing by her side. Mrs. Labee has on a severe gray suit and a white blouse with a big floppy bow. Her back is straight. Her chin is stuck out, as usual. She has the tiniest smile on her face. She keeps her arms at her sides except when she's shaking hands or hugging one of the girls she likes.

Donna's voice is close to my ear. "You can do this, Sue," she whispers. We move along in the line.

"Sue, I'm sure you'll miss Mrs. Labee." It's Miss Hartford talking. "What would you like to say to her?"

I stare at Mrs. Labee. I look at her face, her eyes. I don't say anything. Mrs. Labee doesn't put her hand out to me. I don't reach for her. We just lock eyes with all the bad feelings we have for each other. Finally I turn and walk away from her, away from the line, away from the rec room, and go up the stairs.

The new one

We have a bunch of different housemothers for a while. Mostly we get Miss Rosa, who walks with a limp and tells us that "Home girls are nothing but trouble." She makes it real clear that nothing good can come from Home girls.

One day, when I'm already most of the way through eighth grade, Mac comes into the cottage and calls to us from the foot of the stairs.

"Girls, I have some news for you. Come down here, please. It won't take long."

We come from all directions, mostly from upstairs, and end up in a bunch in the hallway. I'm on one end, Donna's on the other. Mac's standing by the mud room door. He still has his jacket on.

"I wanted to tell you myself that you're going to have a new housemother. Her name is Maude." He checks his notepad. "She'd like to be called Miss Maude."

"Is she from the Bible Seminary?" It's one of the newer girls asking. She smokes a lot, and I think she drinks sometimes, too. Right now, she cracks her gum.

"No," Mac says, looking at the girl. "She's a widow who has raised a number of children on her own. And she's looking forward to being in Cottage No. 3."

A week passes. Almost every day, we ask Miss Rosa if she knows when Miss Maude is coming. She just gives us a superior expression, like she's better than we are, and tells us it will "all come in God's time." This makes me want to spit.

Mac is standing in the hall right next to the door to the mud room. He has a big grin, almost as big as he gets at Christmas when the Masons come and we have a huge party.

"Girls, I'm honored to introduce you to Miss Maude."

He opens the door and a woman pokes her head around the corner. She's got curly grayish-white hair and bright, snappy blue eyes. When she steps into the hall, I can see she doesn't look anything like Mrs. Labee. She's round and smiles a lot. She looks like somebody's grandmother.

We all gather around her while she tells us why she's come to the Home. I stay toward the back, but close enough to hear. She tells us about her husband and how he worked for the railroad, and how they had six children. I watch her hands whirl around while she talks. Maybe she's nervous. There are a lot of us, and she's new at this.

Then she says, "But now my kids are grown up and my husband has passed away, so I've come to take care of you girls."

I look around for Mac. He's part way out the door already. He turns to wave good-bye to all of us. He smiles at me and gives me some kind of salute, like he's saying "Here's a good one for you, kid." He pulls the door closed behind him. I hope he's right.

Soon after she settles in, I know Miss Maude isn't like Miss Hartford and Miss Rosa. For one thing, she smokes. The first time she sits in the living room and lights up a cigarette, we all stand and gawk. She carries a little metal ashtray around with her.

I watch her a lot. I'm waiting, but I'm not sure for what. She likes to wear a button-up sweater, the kind called a cardigan, over a print dress. The first week she's here, she bakes a chocolate cake and, another time, she makes a really good apple pie. She seems really happy when she's baking. I'm nervous about her, that's for sure. But for the first time since I got here almost two years ago, I start sleeping through the night.

One afternoon, a few weeks after Miss Maude's arrival, I'm heading toward the stairs to the rec room when Miss Maude calls me into the living room.

"Sue, can you come here a minute?"

I turn and head straight for her. She's in that brown chair, and smoke is circling up toward the ceiling.

"Would you go down to the store for me, dear? I'm out of powdered sugar."

I'd been to the store for her once before. We need a signed pass to leave the grounds and there's never time to get one to run to the store. But Miss Maude says going to the store is "what kids do," so she sends us anyway. And powdered sugar means she's baking something.

"Sure," I tell her. "I'll go."

"Oh, and Sue, while you're there, I'd like you to get me one more thing."

I wait. She's looking at me like she's assessing something, sort of figuring it out.

"Would you bring me a skyhook, please?" she asks. Her eyes are bright, and they sparkle like she has a secret.

"What's that?" I ask her.

"Oh, the man in the store will know." She holds out a dollar. I nod and stuff it in my pocket and head out the door.

Boy, I hope the old man in the store knows what a skyhook is. And I sure hope I have enough money. When I was there last time, he warned me, "No credit for Home kids."

Sometimes when I get off the property and walk past the regular houses, I pretend I don't live at the Home. Today, the trees along the street are thick and green, and the air smells like it's almost summer. I pick a handful of leaves and spread them out in my hand so they look like a bouquet, like you'd have if you were a bride. Pretty soon, I'm swinging along with my leaf bouquet and singing "Come On-A My House" and pretending I'm Rosemary Clooney.

It's warm and dark inside the store. It's so quiet, I guess I'm the only one getting anything. I hurry to the back shelves where they keep the powdered sugar. I quick find the box and carry it up to the counter. Sure enough, the same man is working here. He looks at me, then he looks at the sugar. I hold the dollar up so he can see it.

"I'll take this powdered sugar, please. It's for Miss Maude." I say this kind of loud as I put the box on the counter. I want him to know it's okay that I'm in the store. "Oh, and Miss Maude wants something else."

"What's that, if I might ask?" He talks slow, like maybe he's from the South.

I feel stupid trying to buy something I never heard of, but I say it anyway.

"She wants a skyhook," I announce. I wait for him to go in the back and get this skyhook thing. I want to see what it is.

"So," he says this real quiet. Then he shakes his head and looks down at the floor. "Miss Maude wants a skyhook, does she?"

I step back. Uh oh, maybe this is something bad.

Now his shoulders are shaking. When he lifts his head, it sounds like he's puffing, but he's laughing. He slaps his skinny brown hand on the counter. "A skyhook," he declares. "Now that's a good one."

I quick turn toward the door. Why did Miss Maude ask me to get this darned skyhook anyway? I want to get out of there.

"Sue. Your name's Sue, right?" I turn around and nod. Geez, he remembers me.

"Sue, there ain't no such thing as a skyhook. It's an old joke. Probably even older than Miss Maude." He smiles a crinkly smile and rests his hands on the counter. "She's pulling your leg, girl. Just funnin' you, that's all." He leans over the counter and hands me the box. "Now take your powdered sugar and go. No charge. And you tell Miss Maude for me that there's a skyhook in that box, sure as shootin', and she'll understand."

I hike back to the cottage carrying the powdered sugar. What does this mean? Mrs. Labee was so hard on me, and now Miss Maude is sending me out for make-believe things. I try not to think about it too much.

When I get to the cottage, Miss Maude is sitting in the living room in her favorite chair, the round brown one they call overstuffed. She's got her menthol cigarettes beside her on the little table. When I see the girls gathered around her waiting for me, I feel like I'm being set up. Like Mrs. Labee is back.

I hand over the box and give her back the dollar. Then I turn away and start toward the stairs.

"What's this for?" she calls after me waving the dollar.

I stop and tell her about the man in the store and what he said about the skyhook. "He says to tell you there's one in the box. That you'd understand."

She gives me a big smile, her eyes bright and shiny. The girls are all laughing and slapping hands and stuff.

"Sue, dear, it was all a bit of fun." She reaches for my hand. "I thought maybe you had a sense of humor hiding in there somewhere." She stands up and parts my bangs so they don't cover my eyes. I look at her, my face serious and closed.

"Well, maybe this was a little too soon," she says and pats me on the shoulder.

Later that evening, we all sit around the dining table eating Miss Maude's yellow layer cake. I think about Mrs. Labee. She never made us cake. And if she had, I would have been afraid to eat it.

I sit next to Donna, and we lick the yummy chocolate powdered sugar icing off our fingers.

"Hey Donna," I whisper. "What the hell is a skyhook?"

She shrugs, and we laugh and eat more cake.

Bring your underwear

When July gets here, I turn fourteen. Miss Maude bakes me my favorite chocolate cake, and then she tells me it's time to get baptized. It's not my idea of a birthday party, especially one where you turn fourteen, but it's what everybody does.

"It's important, Sue. It's part of being in the Home and being a member of the Baptist church."

Home kids spend a lot of time at the church. We go at least twice on Sundays and then a lot of weeknights for Bible classes and potluck suppers. It's pretty boring.

"You'll do fine," she declares. "And we can talk about it later."

It's noisy at our church. The minister hollers. The choir sings loud, and people raise their voices a lot, especially at us Home kids. They tell us to stop doing whatever it is we are doing, behave ourselves, praise Jesus, don't slouch, and stop smoking in the downstairs bathroom. I don't tell anyone, but some of the smokers are the older Girl Scouts who do it after their meetings in the church basement.

We have baptism rehearsals using real water. There are eight of us. I'm the only one from the Home. The pool is way up in the front of the church. It's behind sliding doors. They open the doors for the ceremony. The pool is round, maybe eight feet across, and you have to step down into it. There are two big steps that go all around the inside. A church lady gives us black robes to wear that zip up the front. Our feet are bare. She tells us, "Leave your underwear on under your robes. And make sure you bring extra underwear to church so you'll have something dry to put on after." It's pretty embarrassing to bring a bra and panties to church, but Miss Maude loans me a little bag like a purse to carry them.

In rehearsal, the lady who helps the minister gives us directions about how to go into the pool. When it's my turn, I stand right next to the edge like she says. She puts her hand on my shoulder. The minister is already in the pool with water that looks like it's up to his knees.

"Susan Pickering?" He hollers like I'm way in the back of the church.

"Look him in the eye," the lady whispers. So I do.

"Do you take Jesus Christ to be your savior?"

"I do," I answer, which is what the Sunday school teacher told us to say. I feel silly, like I'm getting married.

When the lady lets go of my shoulder, I put my bare foot on the top step. The water is nice and warm. The minister comes toward me and reaches up to take my hand. By the time I get to the second step, the water is almost up to my knees. Then, when I'm on the bottom of the pool, the water is all the way up to my waist. By now, my robe is starting to blow up like a balloon. With my free hand, I try to bat it down. I can't see the minister over my blown up robe, but I can sure hear his voice.

"Praise God, Susan Pickering, as you enter these baptismal waters," he thunders and pulls me toward him. The girl who's in line behind me starts to giggle. Boy, I bet she can see my underpants. I try to yank my hand away from the minister, but he hangs on tight and hauls me to the center of the pool.

When he dunks me, my robe gets wet and finally sinks down. The church lady helps me out of the pool on the other side and gives me a towel so I can dry off before I go get my other underwear and put on my clothes. I bet even the church lady is trying not to laugh.

On Sunday, when it's time for the real baptism, Miss Maude tells me she'll be coming to the church for the ceremony. That makes me feel good.

"And we can talk about this afterward," she adds.

"Okay," I tell her. Boy, I hope my robe stays put.

Like before, we leave our underwear on and step into our long black robes and zip them up the front. The ushers line us up behind a curtain in the entryway at the back of the church. I peek around the edge to see inside. The room is packed with people, and they're all staring up at the minister. He's up front hanging on to the edges of the pulpit, his eyes are closed, and he's talking real loud to Jesus. When he stops speaking, the organist starts to play. The music sounds real official. One of the ushers, an older boy who goes to high school, pulls back the curtain.

"Get ready," he whispers. The church lady nods at us encouragingly. When the choir starts to sing, the usher motions us to start walking. We go down the aisle, slow and orderly. I'm the fourth one.

Shall we gather at the river,
Where bright angel feet have trod,
With its crystal tide forever
Flowing by the throne of God?

The music is all around us and so strong, I feel like this is a special place to be. I look around until I see Miss Maude and Donna and some of the other girls from our cottage. Miss Maude smiles at me and gives a little wave. Donna is grinning. She did this last year.

I turn back and look toward the front of the church. I keep my back straight and hold my robe to make sure I don't trip over it. I want to do this right.

That's when I see Mom.

She's sitting on the aisle. Les is beside her. They're about ten feet in front of me. My mind is racing around. Why are they here? I haven't seen her since school let out for the summer. I hardly told her anything about this.

I walk slowly, keeping in step with the other kids. The choir sings like it's a big celebration. My heart is beating really fast.

As the line begins to pass her, Mom turns around. She's looking at me, and she's crying. Her bright red lipstick makes a crooked line around her mouth. Tears make streaks through the rouge on her cheeks. I take another step, and she reaches back toward me, like she's trying to touch me, her fingers stretched out in the air.

The people sitting near the aisle look at her, then at me. I take another step. I'm so close now that, even over the sound of the choir, I can hear her crying. I see her hand trying to touch the sleeve of my robe. I take a deep breath. Then I reach out and squeeze her fingers. It's like hello.

Finally our line arrives at the front of the church, and all eight of us are standing by the pool. I try not to, but all I can think about is Mom. I watch the first three being baptized. Now it's my turn. I stand on the edge like we did during practice and wait for the minister to call my name. I know the whole room will hear it. Mom will hear it.

"Susan Pickering." He sings it out loud and clear.

I hold my breath and step down into the water. This time my robe begins to sink like it's supposed to. I go slowly down the steps and feel the warm water rise all the way up to my waist. Now it's time to put my hand in the hand of the minister and bow my head.

His voice rings out.

"I baptize you in the name of the Father, and of the Son, and of the Holy Ghost."

I close my eyes. When this is over, I have to do something about Mom.

Talking it over

Miss Maude and I are sitting in the living room. I'm on one end of the couch, and she's on the other. It's dark outside. One of the sliding windows is open, and a cool night breeze comes in every once in a while.

"She didn't wait for you after church?" Miss Maude asks.

I don't answer right away. We've been talking about Mom and how she came to the baptism this morning. It's hard. I don't even talk to Mac about things like this.

I kick my slippers off and fold my legs under me on the couch.

"They were already gone when I got outside."

There I was carrying Miss Maude's purse with my wet underwear in it, trying to figure out what I'd say to them, and they weren't there. I walked up to the corner looking for Les's big gray car, just to be sure. I even sat on the church steps for a while, in case they'd gone to Tony the Greek's for coffee and would come looking for me.

"I waited for a while. But they didn't come back."

Miss Maude nods. It's quiet again.

"Do you want to call her, Sue?"

"No."

"You're upset, I know. Can you talk about it?"

I let out a big sigh and move over by the window. Even when I can't see much outside, being near a window helps me think about hard stuff. I watch tree leaves flicker in the streetlight near the cottage.

"I don't know what to do. She gets like this, and I'm embarrassed." I lower my voice. "I just want a mom I can be close to."

Even before I finish saying all that, the tears start. I sniffle and try to hold them back. Miss Maude stretches her hand out to me. She's holding a tissue.

I walk over and take it, then I plunk down on the couch by her side.

"I know, Sue, it's not easy for you to have your mom do things like this. And I know it wasn't easy when you went to live with them, and you and your mom had that fight."

I turn and stare at her. "You know about that?"

She nods.

Now I feel even more embarrassed. If she knows all this stuff, how could she think I'm a special girl? How the hell could that be?

"Who told you?"

"Mac did, dear." She looks at me like she's trying to figure things out. "You know, Sue, he loves you like a daughter. And he thinks about you a lot. He wanted me to know enough so that I could help out, if need be." Her voice is drifting away like she's said too much.

My insides are whirling around like a washing machine. I know that awful Mrs. Labee didn't know about the fight. But Mac figures he could tell Miss Maude. She said he cares about me. And she cares about me, too.

I stare at the floor. "Do you think I should call my mom?"

More silence. Then, "No, honey, I don't think that's necessary. When do you see her again?"

"Pretty soon, I guess. Sometimes we meet at Woolworth's at the counter for a soda or something."

"Well, Sue, how about you let a little time pass. It seems like sometimes your mom isn't ready to talk about things."

By now I'm watching Miss Maude's face, her eyes. I need to see the truth. "Do I wait for her to call about meeting? We usually do it after school, but now it's summer."

Miss Maude thinks about it. "I guess so, Sue. Sometimes it's really hard to know what to do in situations like this. You know?"

I nod. "I think I'll go to bed now," I tell her.

She smiles. "You were wonderful today during your baptism. I was so proud of you."

"Thanks." I stand up ready to go upstairs. "Oh. I'll dry out your little bag and get it back to you in the morning."

She stands and stretches out her arms. "Good night, dear heart."

I step into her hug, feeling the warmth of her solid arms around me. You can trust her, I tell myself. It's okay.

Les calls me during the week to let me know Mom's "not feeling well."

"What's wrong with her? I mean, is it a cold or something?" I feel stupid asking this, but I don't know what else to say.

"No, Sue. It's just that, well, she's been upset lately, and you know how she gets."

I think about the baptism, about her messed up makeup, her tears, her hand reaching out to me. "Yeah," I tell him. "I know how she gets."

It's almost a month before I'm sitting beside her at the counter at Woolworths. Her eyes are clear, and she's telling stories and laughing. I'm afraid if we talk about the baptism and stuff, it will send her off again. So I sip my soda and giggle at her stories and try to forget.

Home girl earns bus tokens

In September I start ninth grade at North High. All the Home kids go here, at least until they leave the Home or drop out. It's mostly a vocational school, but some kids take college prep courses. That's what I want to do. I just try not to think about how on earth I could even get into college. I want so much to go, but I don't know where I'd get the money. Or whether a college would accept a Home girl. Thinking about it drives me crazy.

When I graduated from eighth grade, I was the salutatorian, a long word for being second in the class. Miss Maude asked me, "Are you planning on taking college courses in high school?" When I shrugged my shoulders, she said, "You should, you know. Don't let that mind of yours go to waste."

I've only been at North High for about a week when the principal moves me ahead to the second half of ninth grade. That means, when I'm in twelfth grade, I'll be graduating in January, not in June. There will only be around 90 kids graduating in my group, while the regular class has about 500. Most of the 90 kids were kept back, but a few, like me, skipped a term. Kids in the regular class laugh at us and call us the "in-betweens."

As soon as school starts, Mac announces that the Montgomery Ward department store gave the Home a whole bunch of winter coats. The housemothers are pretty excited until they find out they're all black leather jackets. Most of the kids think it's cool, especially the guys. I figure regular people didn't buy them because they didn't want their kids to look like troublemakers. Or like Home kids.

When it's my turn to pick one, Miss Maude and I go up to the storage room in the Main Building. I search through the pile of jackets with her until we find one that sort of fits. The leather squeaks when I put it on. Right away I make a face about the rabbit's foot that's hanging from the zipper.

"It's fake, honey," Miss Maude assures me. "You don't need to worry."

"I know, but I don't want to touch it every time I have to wear this."

I look in the mirror. My straight dark brown hair comes down to my shoulders. On top, all you can see is this huge black leather jacket with lots of zippers and enormous shoulders. I'm wearing my faded old poodle skirt, and my skinny legs stick out the bottom, ending in thin white socks and dirty brown lace-up shoes. When I move, there's a flash of red satin lining from inside the jacket.

I turn and face Miss Maude. "This is *not* cool."

"Don't complain, Sue. That jacket will keep you warm when you're walking home from school this winter." She has a serious look on her face when she tells me this.

North High is a couple of miles from the Home, and we only get one bus token a day. Mostly I ride to school in the morning so I won't be late. Then I have to walk home in the afternoon, which is a drag.

Every day on my way to school, I take off my ugly brown shoes and stick them under a huge bush that's right on the edge of Home property. Then I dig around in the pile of sneakers we keep out of site under that same bush to find mine. Lots of times they're sort of wet, but it's better than going to high school looking like an old lady. There are so many shoes and sneakers under the bush, the Home kids call it the Endicott Johnson shoe store, just like the real shops around town.

The students at the high school pretty much stay away from Home kids. For the first month or so, I hang out a lot with Donna. I don't say very much, not even in class. The darn jacket doesn't help, that's for sure. I sure hate wearing it, but it's getting cold and rainy, and Miss Maude's right, the jacket keeps me warm and kind of dry. Boy, I wish I had more bus tokens.

One morning I'm standing just inside the door at Tony the Greek's, waiting for the bus. A lot of high school kids from this side of town hang out here. Tony doesn't like it when Home kids come inside because we don't have any money. But sometimes when it's cold or rainy, Tony ignores us if we stand right inside the door and don't get too loud.

This morning, I'm watching some guys play pool. They do this a lot. Some of them go to North High. My eyes get big when I see a tall, skinny guy plunk down a dollar, maybe more, on the edge of the pool table. Whoa. Does that mean they play for money sometimes? I look away and think about this. If I could play and win some money, I could buy bus tokens! That's it. I'm going to learn how to play pool.

The next morning, I walk right up to the pool table. I don't let myself think about it, I just do it. The guys stop for a minute and stare. I guess maybe I look pretty weird in my black leather jacket, my boring cotton dress, and my wet sneakers. But I stand right next to the pool table anyway and watch them play.

The next few mornings, I spend about half an hour before the bus comes standing beside that pool table. I watch how the boys hit the balls with the long stick. I check out how they hang over the edge of the table to make a shot. Sometimes they rub what looks like blue chalk on the end of the stick. That must make it work better.

Finally, one morning a tall skinny boy nods at me. He keeps a cigarette in his mouth almost all the time. The smoke goes right up in his eyes and makes him squint, but he plays good pool anyway. His fingers are brown on the ends like Mom's.

"You play?" he asks. His voice sounds kind of lazy, like maybe he's not from around here.

I take a quick look out the window. The other Home kids are already getting on the bus.

"No," I answer. "But I want to learn."

He stares in my eyes for what feels like a long time. I don't blink.

"Well, this here's a cue," he says holding out the long stick. He motions to me with his head to follow him around the table. For once, I'm up close enough to really see how he makes his shots.

The next few mornings, I spend the half hour before the bus comes hanging out right behind him. I watch him put all the balls inside a little wooden triangle. I see him circle the table, then pick his spot. Sometimes he rests his hip against the edge and leans over to hit a ball with the cue. He studies things a lot.

After about a week, he goes over to the case on the wall and gets a pool cue. He holds it out to me.

"I'm Frankie," he says.

"Sue," I answer. I take the cue. It's light and smooth. My heart starts going fast. I'm on my way!

"Home kid?"

"Yeah."

He nods and turns back to the table.

Frankie tells me what moves to make, what ball to hit next, where to stand. His voice is low, sort of flat. No one pays much attention to us. His friends look at us sometimes like it's pretty weird, him teaching me to play pool, but they leave us alone. Then after a few weeks, Frankie calls to one of his buddies.

"Hey, Johnny. Come play a game with Sue here."

"She any good?" Johnny smirks.

Frankie shrugs. Everybody laughs. My heart starts to climb right up into my throat. I try not to turn bright red.

Johnny has curly black hair and dark brown eyes. He swaggers toward me with a little grin on his face. Right then, everything I learned from Frankie flies out of my head.

Frankie passes his cue stick to me and walks to the lunch counter, leaving us alone by the table.

"Hey. I'm Johnny."

"I'm Sue."

He starts to rack the balls. "Eight ball, yeah?"

I nod.

"So what are we playing for, Sue?"

I take a deep breath. "Money. For bus tokens."

Johnny turns toward me and starts to laugh.

"Bus tokens?" He looks around at the guys. Now they're all laughing.

"Yeah. I need to buy bus tokens," I tell him.

"Okay." He looks at me for a minute, like he's figuring something out. "So, you don't have any money, right?" I nod. "So if I win, what do I get?"

By now, at least a dozen kids are crowded around us. I hold up a brown paper bag. "My lunch."

Boy, that really gets them going. They're slapping each other on the back and banging each other on the arm. I feel my face get all hot. It must sound pretty stupid, wanting money for bus tokens. But I guess Johnny doesn't know what it's like to walk over a mile to or from North High in the cold slush all winter. Maybe he doesn't go to school.

When I lose, I hand Johnny my lunch, grab my leather jacket and start for the door. Frankie appears beside me and slips me a bus token.

"Use it. You're late."

"Yeah. Sorry." I'm embarrassed, but Frankie doesn't seem to mind.

"See you tomorrow?" he asks. I nod.

The lessons last all winter. And I start to win. Pretty soon I'm riding the bus both ways.

I know I can't keep my pool playing from Miss Maude forever. She's too smart. One day when I get home from school, she asks me how I'm getting back and forth, what with after school activities and all. I take a deep breath.

"I learned to play pool down at Tony the Greek's. You know, the coffee shop by the bus stop?" I look her in the eye. "I play for money." She stares at me, waiting for me to say more. "I needed the money to buy tokens so I could ride the bus to school and back. I win games now. A lot. Well, enough to buy tokens anyway."

Miss Maude throws her head back and lets out a big laugh. She claps her hands together. "Bless you, Sue Pickering, this is good news. I knew you could figure out how to take care of yourself."

"Then it's all right if I play pool for money? I mean, so I can buy tokens?"

"Of course. As long as you take care of yourself." She looks at me and now, her face is serious. "Sue, dear one, you're like a bright penny, but you don't know it yet." She pushes my dark brown bangs to one side and taps me in the middle of my forehead. "You're going to make it. You've got a lot going on in here."

Caroling

It's winter now which means it's cold and snow is piled up everywhere, and I'm using my bus tokens a lot.

"Well, for heaven's sake, Sue, go read what's posted on the bulletin board." That's what Miss Maude says when I complain there's nothing to do around here for Christmas.

The invitation is decorated with red and green drawings of bells and candles. I go up close to read. It says a hospital wants us to come and sing for people who can't go home for Christmas. I sign up. I like to sing. Plus it gets me off Home grounds for a while.

Miss Hartford is our song leader. We practice Christmas carols until we can do two or three verses without looking in the book. It reminds me of singing with Mom. Sometimes, when I was 9 or

10, long before I came here, I'd be in the bathtub and Mom would sit on the edge. As she washed my back, we'd sing hymns together. I liked "Abide with Me." Mom always sang the melody and I did the alto part.

"What do I wear?" I ask Miss Maude.

"Get dressed like you're going to church."

I put on a plaid school skirt and a button-up sweater. At the last minute, I put on my good black shoes, even though it's snowing.

"Are you coming?"

"No. I need to stay home. Some girls aren't going. Besides, it would be too much walking for an old lady." She smiles.

"Have fun, dears," she calls as Donna and I go out the front door. "There'll be a treat waiting when you get home."

We climb onto a big bus like the one you take to go downtown. Miss Hartford is already sitting up front next to another housemother. She looks excited. By the time we leave for the hospital, every seat is full.

I look out the window as the bus pulls away. The cottage door is closed and it's dark, but I wave anyway, just in case Miss Maude is watching.

All the way to the hospital, we sing. The bus driver leaves the lights on inside so we can watch Miss Hartford when she stands up to direct us. It feels like we're in church except we're moving. She blows on her pitch pipe and then waves her hands to help us keep time. Her cheeks are pink and her eyes sparkle. I've never seen her like this before.

It's warm in the bus. I sit beside Donna, who is already 15 and is still taller than I am. The light bounces off her glasses whenever she turns her head. I've never asked her, but I wonder what her family is like. Home kids don't talk about that much. I haven't seen her go off the grounds with anyone, and she doesn't say anything about a mom or a dad.

After a whole bunch of hymns, Donna nudges me. "We're here," she whispers and nods toward the window. There's a big lighted sign that says "Hospital."

The bus turns into the driveway. Snow is piled along the sides of the narrow pavement like a snowplow went through not long ago. The bus stops in front of a big brick building. It's pretty dark out, but there are lights by the stairs.

"Time to go, girls."

Miss Hartford waits outside the bus and inspects us as we get off.

"Button your coat, Sue," she says as I pass her. "And everyone remember to be very quiet. There are sick people inside."

The light over the tall front doors makes them shine like gold. There's a sign on the building beside the doors, but it's hard to see. I go closer. It says "Binghamton State Hospital."

I turn around and hurry back toward the bus. My head is dizzy. I want to cry. When I stay beside the bus, Donna comes over to me and touches my arm.

"Sue, what's wrong?" she whispers. "Are you okay?"

I shake my head.

Girls walk past us. Miss Hartford is standing tall by the hospital doors, holding one of them open. She keeps glancing back at me. Donna leans close to my ear and whispers, "Are you going to throw up?" I shake my head again. I hold on to her arm, and we walk over to the building. I look down as we go up the stairs, past Miss Hartford and into the hospital. The whole way I hold tight to Donna's arm.

We're all standing in what looks like an entryway. There's not much light. After my head stops spinning, I lean close to Donna. "This is where they brought my mom." Her eyes grow big behind her glasses. Donna looks around. "They kept her in here for a long time. Mom hated this place." I keep my voice low. "She says they made her have electric shock or something. It made her real sick."

It's quiet inside the entryway, even with a whole bunch of girls jammed in here. Ahead of us is a long hallway. A woman in a white uniform stands at the end of the hall, next to a large wooden door. She is holding a bunch of keys.

Miss Hartford turns to face us. "Girls," she calls in a soft voice. Nobody makes a sound.

"We're going to start singing now. The nurse will open each door for us, and then lock it behind us once we're all inside." The nurse nods.

Donna and I look at each other. Lock us inside?

"Remember, girls, we're here to help the less fortunate celebrate Christmas." She's talking quietly, but it's her cheery voice. "We'll begin with 'The First Noel.'" She sounds our note on the pitch pipe and lifts her hands to lead us. When she swings her arms, we start to sing. Miss Hartford whirls her hands around. That means sing louder.

We walk down the hallway slowly, sort of in time to the music. The nurse unlocks the heavy door at the end, pulls it open and stands back against the door to let us pass. When we're all on the other side, she comes in and closes and locks the door behind us. The only light comes from a row of dim bulbs way up high on the walls. I look around. It's another long dark hall. It's empty, just like the last one. Miss Hartford holds up one finger. That means sing the first verse again.

The first Noel the angel did say
Was to certain poor shepherds in fields as they lay

The nurse hurries past us rattling her keys in the pale light. I watch her unlock the next door.

Now we begin our slow walk into a large room. It's even darker than the hall. Our voices sound small in this big space. There are so many beds, it looks kind of like the dorm back in Orton.

It's warm in here. As we sing, I unbutton my coat and look around. Some women are staying close to the walls. A few look over at us, but not for long. There are some small windows up high by the ceiling. The women are wearing nightgowns, or maybe robes. I try not to stare, but I want to see.

"Your mom was in *here*?" Donna whispers.

I nod.

When I hear the pitch pipe for another song, I look at Donna. "'We Three Kings,'" she whispers.

We three kings of orient are.
Bearing gifts, we traverse afar.

The nurse keeps unlocking and locking doors. We move in a line from one big dark room to the next. Boy, being inside this place feels creepy. Donna stays close beside me. I can tell she wants to ask questions. "We'll talk later," I whisper to her between carols.

After about an hour, we end up in a cafeteria where some women are working behind a counter. The room has lots of metal tables and chairs, and they're all empty. No one else is in here. The ladies smile as they pour paper cups of apple juice for us. It's cold, and it tastes really good.

As we sit down and drink our juice, the nurse stands and talks to us. "I'm sure everyone appreciated your fine singing," she says. I look at Donna and roll my eyes. For the first time that night, we giggle.

"Now girls, there will be one last stop before you return to your bus." We finish our juice and the nurse has us line up in another hallway in front of another locked door. Donna and I are at the back of the line. "We're about to go into the girls' ward," she announces. Her voice sounds different, like it's official. "Stay in order and do your best job. The girls here have been wanting to hear you sing."

There's a girls' ward? I look at Donna. Her eyes are as big as mine.

Miss Hartford stops us in the hallway next to the door. While the nurse uses one of her big keys to open the door, Miss Hartford gives us the pitch for "Oh Little Town of Bethlehem." When the door is open, our little choir files past the nurse and enters the girls' room.

Oh little town of Bethlehem,
How still we see thee lie.

As soon as I step inside the room, I see her. There's a long row of beds, and a girl is standing near them not far from the door. I nudge Donna with my elbow. "Look," I whisper. I stare at the girl to show Donna where to look. We slow down.

"Wasn't she at the Home?" I ask in a quiet voice. The rest of the choir keeps on singing and moving slowly through the room.

Donna nods. That's when I slide my hand into Donna's and squeeze tightly.

"What's her name?" I keep my voice real low.

"I think it's Crystal. She wasn't there very long."

When Donna says the name, the girl turns her head our way a little. Then she begins to rock slowly from side to side in time to our singing. She looks like she's sort of asleep.

The hopes and fears of all the years . . .

"Crystal, is that you?" I say this so soft, I can hardly hear my own voice.

She flicks her fingers just a bit, like she hears me. But she doesn't look at me.

How could a girl from the Home be in this place? What does this mean? It makes my stomach hurt, just to think about it.

I feel Miss Hartford's hand grip my shoulder.

"Sue," she says, her voice quiet but steady. "You need to stay with the group. Don't get distracted."

"It's Crystal," I say to her. "Crystal is in here." My hands ball up like fists.

Miss Hartford pauses for a second like she's about to say something. Then she shakes her head, touches my arm and steers me toward the singing Home girls. I look back, but the girl has disappeared in the shadows.

When we get home, the cottage is filled with delicious smells, and Miss Maude has the big table in the dining room loaded with red and green decorated cookies and cocoa.

"These will help you get warm," she announces. She sounds lively. "Now, tell me all about the caroling. What did you sing?"

The girls begin to grab cookies and tell stories. After a while, Miss Maude goes into the kitchen to fill the pitcher with more cocoa. I follow her.

"What kind of a hospital is it, where we were tonight?" I ask her.

She stops stirring the cocoa on the stove and turns around. She looks in my eyes for a minute, no smile or anything.

"It's called a mental hospital, Sue. People go there when they aren't able to take care of themselves. When they have problems."

"Can't take care of themselves?" I wait for a moment. I'm scared about what I'm going to hear, but I ask anyway. "What does that mean?"

"You remember, Sue, back when your mom was sick?" Miss Maude speaks slowly, like she's thinking things through. "She had a lot of problems back then. She couldn't take care of herself very well. Or you."

Somehow, she knows what happened.

I turn away. I don't want to hear her say any more. I run upstairs into my room and find my pajamas. I don't put them on. I just sit on the edge of my bed in the dark and stare out the window.

The call

I'm up in my room, fussing around with my math homework. Somebody's playing "Mr. Sandman" on the radio. The girls are laughing and singing along. It's still chilly outside but it's almost spring. And this summer, it'll be three years since I came here. It feels like forever.

"Sue, your mom's on the phone." It's Miss Maude calling me. I can tell she's in the hallway downstairs.

Mom hardly ever calls me. When Miss Maude hands me the phone, she gives me an "I hope everything's okay" look. Not long after she got here, Miss Maude put a brown plastic chair in the hallway close to the phone. That way, you can sit down while you talk. Mrs. Labee never did that.

"Mom? Hi."

"Sue, dear. How are you?"

"I'm fine, Mom." I wait but she doesn't say anything more. "Mom? Is everything okay?"

When she starts crying, I sit down.

"What happened, Mom?"

No answer.

"Are you at home?"

I don't know why I ask that. I can't imagine where she'd be except at home. But I ask anyway.

"Sue, can you meet me tomorrow? After school? I need . . . to ask you something."

Her words don't sound right. It's like she has a sock in her mouth.

"What's wrong, Mom?"

"It's my teeth." She takes a deep breath. "They're broken."

I turn away from the hallway. I don't want the girls to hear about this.

"Your teeth? You mean your false teeth? How did they get broken?" I'm whispering.

There's a big pause. I hear Mom sniffling. She blows her nose.

"Never mind, Mom." I close my eyes. Les is a foot taller than Mom and at least fifty pounds heavier. Not long ago, when Mom and I met downtown after school, she had a bruise on her cheek. I didn't ask about it.

"I need to have my . . . teeth . . . fixed. Or maybe I'll need new ones." She inhales. It's a deep sound, like it hurts.

"Sue? I hate to ask you this, but do you have any money?" She's never asked me this before.

I'm scattered, but I try to figure out in my head how much money I have. I get a little for cleaning the mud room. Miss Maude keeps that in her lock box. And I have my bus token money. It's in a sock in a drawer under my pajamas. Miss Maude knows where it is, but we don't talk about it.

"How much will it cost, Mom?"

"I don't know yet. I see the dentist in the morning."

I think about how to do this.

"Okay, Mom. I'll meet you at the soda fountain at Woolworths after school tomorrow. Around 3:30. Okay?"

No answer.

"I'll bring whatever money I can. It's not much, but I'll give it to you then, okay?"

"Oh, Sue, I hate to do this. I know you don't have much. And here you are stuck at the Home." I don't say anything. "I'll try to pay you back, honey. But I don't know how long it will be." Her voice sounds like it's going away.

"Don't worry, Mom. It'll be okay." Then I ask, "Is Les home?" I don't know what I can do if he is. Or if he isn't. But I ask anyway.

"Everything is fine, dear. It was only a little flare up."

Only a little flare up? And her teeth are broken?

The next day, when school lets out, I take the bus downtown. I have seventeen dollars zipped in my black leather jacket pocket. It's not a lot, but at least it's something. When I told Miss Maude about Mom's problem, right away she unlocked the money box and handed me the six dollars I had saved. The rest is my bus token money.

Sitting on the bus, I look out the window. The bus goes by regular houses. Then office buildings. I unzip my pocket to make sure I have another token to take the bus home. I lean my head against the window and close my eyes.

Mom used to tell me a story. She told it lots of times. "When you were born, Sue-Sue, the doctor told me I gave you all my calcium. So after that, I lost my teeth." She usually laughed here. "Boy, what a big strong baby you were."

"You were a surprise, coming along after sixteen years. And then, when you were late, your father made me stay in the hospital. I was there for three weeks! He was so worried about us," she told me. She was proud about this.

Mom said she got bored, so they put her to work folding towels in the laundry. "I never saw so many towels," she'd say, laughing.

I finally arrived at 7:15 a.m. on July 16. "It was hotter than sin that morning," Mom would say, shaking her head. "And you were such a big baby! Eight pounds, eleven ounces. But it was all worth it." Next came the teeth part. "It was only a few years later that I had to have all my teeth out." And finally she'd get to the part about my dad. "But by then, Sue-Sue, your father had left us."

I open my eyes. The bus is pulling up across the street from Woolworths. I step off and go to the corner and wait for the light to change. I keep my hand around the seventeen dollars in my pocket.

Mom is already sitting at the counter. She's got a glass of water in front of her. She always has coffee. Maybe water's easier right now. And it doesn't cost anything.

When I sit down on the stool next to her, she turns away. I stare at the counter.

"Can I get you something?"

It's the waitress. She's standing behind the counter, wiping her hands on what looks like a dish towel. She's talking to me, but she's looking at Mom.

"A cola, please. With lemon."

She nods and goes away.

Mom turns to face forward. Her hands are on her glass. She doesn't say anything.

I put the seventeen dollars on the counter close to her.

"It's not very much," I tell her.

She doesn't look.

"What did the dentist say?"

Silence.

"Did you see him?"

She nods. She glances down at the money and turns back to her glass of water. It looks like her cheeks are wet.

"Mom? Are you okay?" I know that's a stupid thing to say, but her silence scares me.

She turns her head slightly in my direction, not all the way, but a little. Then I see a tiny smile. She nods her head, telling me she's okay, I guess. She reaches down by her side. Her purse is on the floor next to her stool. She shifts it to her lap and paws around in it. She takes out a pencil, then reaches for the napkin holder in front of us and pulls out a paper napkin. Smoothing it on the counter, she begins to write.

I want to watch, but I look away. She doesn't want to talk, to open her mouth, to show me she doesn't have any teeth. Maybe the dentist hurt her. I think about all the ugly metal fillings the dentist who works on Home kids put in my mouth. He's always in a hurry, pushing, rushing. Like he doesn't care who we are.

I look at Mom. I hope her dentist is a good one, one who takes care of her. I say a little prayer in my mind. "Take care of her, please. Amen."

She slides the napkin across to me and moves the money closer to her. I pick up the napkin.

"Thank you, Sue-Sue. This helps. Les will pay the rest. ILY Mom"

I'm staring at the napkin when the waitress puts a glass down in front of me. "One cola with lemon. That'll be five cents please."

I rummage through the change that's left in my jacket and pull out a nickel. The waitress tucks it in a little pocket in her apron and goes away.

Mom is buttoning her coat. Her purse is on her lap. The seventeen dollars is gone from the counter.

"Mom? Are you leaving?"

She stands, then turns to me and nods.

"Are you okay?"

She reaches for me. I stand. She wraps her arms around me, resting her head on my shoulder, her purse dangling against my side.

"Oh, Sue-Sue," she says. Her voice is muffled. "I'll call you when I can." I can't really understand the words, but I know what she's saying.

I watch her push open the front door of Woolworths, hurrying, her head down.

RELATIVES

The invitation

"Hey Sue, got a minute?"

It's Mac. He's calling to me from his office window.

"Sure."

I plop down on the grass by the edge of the sidewalk and poke at the blister on my heel. It's only the middle of May, but it's so hot, my T-shirt sticks to my back. I wish I could jump in the river and climb up on the big old wooden float, but we can't go in till after Memorial Day. It's the rule.

Mac comes out of the Main Building through the big front door. "Let's get out of the sun," he says. His forehead is wet, and he looks hot already. We go across the grass and sit on an old bench in the shade. The wood is still warm.

"Glad to be done with school for a while?"

I shake my head. School let out a week ago, and I'm already bored.

"Well, your birthday's coming up, young lady. Fifteen, I believe?"

I smile. Fifteen sounds so cool.

Mac leans back against the bench.

"Sue, has your mom talked much about her brother named Hamilton?"

I stare at my sneakers. Why is Mac asking about Mom's brother?

"I think he lives in Florida. Is that right?" I ask.

Mac nods.

"A long time ago, before kindergarten, Mom and I went there. It was hot, and sand got into everything. They lived on a farm, I think. They had a bunch of turkeys." I make a face.

"Well, Hamilton and his wife—I don't recall her name right now—still live on a little farm outside of Fort Lauderdale. They said it's the same one as before. "

"It's Beulah." I look over at Mac. "Her name is Beulah."

When he doesn't say anything, I ask, "Did something happen to them?"

"Oh no, Sue, everything's fine." He looks surprised. "In fact, I have an invitation for you. Your aunt and uncle called me. They'd like to have you come and stay with them for a while this summer."

He pulls out a dark blue hanky and wipes the sweat off his face.

How did they find me? Did Mom write to them?

"They want to fly you down to Florida. You'd stay with them on their farm, and you'd be pretty near the ocean." He turns and smiles at me. He's heard me talk about how I love being near water. "Well? How does it sound?"

"For how long?"

"Oh, I imagine you'll be back before school starts in the fall."

I think about this. If I say yes, I get to go on an airplane. And swim in the ocean. That could be a lot better than hanging out in the Susquehanna River and having the Home boys push me off the float. But what if Mom's brother drinks a lot and gets crazy-mad like Mom does, and I'm stuck down there? I frown.

"Kind of scary?" Mac asks.

I nod.

"Well, Sue, after your uncle called me, I did some checking, and your aunt and uncle are fine people. They're older, and they never had any children of their own." He waits, but I don't say anything. "I think they'd like to get to know you, that's all." After another pause, he adds, "I don't know this for sure, but they might ask you to stay down there with them."

I turn to him in surprise. Live in Florida with people I don't know, just because they're my aunt and uncle? Does Mom know about this?

"Do I have to? I mean, live with them?"

"No, you certainly don't have to. And you don't have to decide about going right this minute either," Mac tells me. "Why don't you go talk it over with Miss Maude. Then call me or come see me, and let me know."

I get up and with a quick thanks and a wave for Mac, I walk fast down to the cottage. Miss Maude is in the kitchen. I lean on the counter and watch her rinse some lettuce under the faucet.

"Hi," I say.

"Hi back," she answers. "Pretty hot out, huh?"

"Miss Maude?" I wait while she turns the water off. "Mac told me my aunt and uncle called. They live in Florida. He's Mom's older brother." She nods like she already knows. "They want me to come for a visit. This summer."

She dries her hands on a dish towel and turns so she can really see me.

"Do you know about this?" I ask her. I don't take my eyes off her face.

She nods. "A little bit."

Miss Maude comes over to stand beside me. We lean against the kitchen counter.

"What do you think, Sue? Would you like to go?"

I shrug my shoulders.

"What's wrong, dear?"

"What if they decide they don't really want me there? What if they do mean things?" I look away. "Or what if they want to *keep* me down there?" It's hard to talk about stuff like this, but Miss Maude makes it easier somehow.

"Mac wouldn't even consider this if he didn't know they were good people." She tips my chin up so she can see my eyes. "Honey, this is a chance for you. You'll meet some of your relatives. And you'll get to see the ocean. Try not to worry too much, Sue. Just see how it goes."

"But what will I wear down there? A lot of my shorts and stuff are worn out." I don't know why I start talking about clothes.

"How about we shop for a new dress to wear on the plane, and maybe some other things." She looks me up and down, like she's measuring me. "You'll definitely need a new swimsuit. But don't you worry, young lady. Your aunt and uncle are not bringing you all the way to Florida to check out your wardrobe!" She puts her arm across my shoulders. "How soon would you go?" she asks.

The sound of her voice makes me feel safer.

"Pretty soon. In June, I guess." I wait for a minute, then the scary part comes back. "But what if I get there and things are weird and I want to come back early?"

She brushes my bangs out of my eyes.

"Your aunt and uncle sound like lovely people. I'm sure it will work out fine, dear heart. And just think. You'll get to see another part of the world." She squeezes my hand. "And, when you get back, you'll be fifteen!"

I smile. I talk all the time about turning fifteen. That's in July.

I walk upstairs and stare at the phone in the hall. After a while, I pick it up and dial Mac's office.

"Mac? It's me. I talked it over with Miss Maude."

"And?"

"She thinks I should go."

"Well, what do you think, Sue?"

I take a deep breath. "Yeah. I guess so."

Getting to Florida

It's hot and loud in the airplane. Almost every seat is taken. There are even families with little kids going to Florida. After the stewardess learns my name, she keeps coming around and asking me things.

"Want another soda, Sue?"

"Would you like me to turn on the air conditioner? It's warm in here."

"Sue, how about a sandwich?"

She looks so cool in her navy blue and red uniform. She's tall, and her hair is pulled back in a twist. Maybe I could be a stewardess someday.

I rub at the coke spot on my new yellow dress but it doesn't go away. I give up and look out the window. The clouds are soft and fluffy, like in a cartoon. Or like cotton candy. We go right through them. I don't know how we stay up so high. I hug my purse and try not to think about it.

I lean back in my seat and close my eyes.

A few days ago, I said good-bye to Mom at the counter at Woolworths. "I think you'll like Ham," she told me, smiling. Her new teeth were a lot whiter than the old ones. "Hamilton is his real name, but we've always called him Ham." She took a sip of her coffee. "There were four of us. He was the oldest. I was the baby. You and I stayed with him and Beulah when we went to Florida." She shook her head. "That was such a long time ago. You were four, I think. Do you remember?"

I nodded.

She opened her eyes wide. "His eyes are the same color as mine."

Mom's eyes are golden. So are mine, sort of.

"Beulah's a bit different," Mom said, stirring her coffee. She looked away, like she was remembering. "She's not as easy to be around as your Uncle Ham. But she means well." She turned to me and grinned. "She's short and round. I think of her as sturdy."

"Have you always written letters to them? I mean, like you did this time, about me going down there?"

"Well, not always." She shook her head. "We lost touch."

Pause. I waited.

"I was hoping maybe you could get to know them Sue, even if only for a little while. After all, we don't have much family."

We sat in silence sipping our drinks, me with a soda and Mom with her coffee, listening to the ringing sounds of cash registers.

"Mom? Was Uncle Ham nice to you when you were growing up?"

"Oh my, yes." She laughed. "Ask him to tell you the story about me and the lemon juice. He'll get a kick out of that."

I open my eyes and slide the packet with my airline ticket out of my purse. It says I go back to Binghamton on Saturday, the 25th of August. That's a little more than two months away. How do I spend this much time with people I don't even know? My mind flops around. Don't worry so much, Sue, I tell myself. I take off my new tan flats with the little leather bows on the front and curl up on the seat. Whatever happens, I guess I'll figure it out.

Uncle Ham and Aunt Beulah

By the time the plane lands in Miami, my new dress has soda stains, mustard spots, and a million wrinkles. When we all line up in the aisle and begin to shuffle toward the exit sign, I try to smooth it out, but nothing helps.

"Don't forget your purse, Sue," the stewardess calls to me. I turn around. She's standing by my seat holding up my tan purse. She works her way toward me squeezing past the lined up passengers and hands it to me. I feel my face get hot. "Thank you," I tell her and she grins.

"Have a good vacation," she says. I smile, like I know what that means, and continue to the exit.

The airport is so cold, it's like being inside a huge refrigerator. Lots of people carrying suitcases hurry by me. When I reach the end of the little walkway that leads to the waiting area, I see a tall man waving. He's looking over at me and smiling. He's tan and doesn't have much hair, and his arms look really long. After a few more steps, I notice a short round woman with silvery hair standing beside him. Her button-up-the-front dress has lots of green and white flowers on it. I try one last time to shake the wrinkles out of my tired-looking yellow dress and wave. Soon I'm there.

"Susan! My goodness. It's so good to have you here." It's Aunt Beulah. She sounds friendly but she looks serious.

"Thank you for inviting me, Aunt Beulah," I answer. The image of Miss Maude runs through my mind. "Be polite," she always tells me.

I look up at Uncle Ham. His smile is so wide, I can hardly see his eyes.

"Hi," I say and smile back.

"Welcome," he tells me. He looks happy. Then we all come together in a sort of a hug. It feels strange.

"Let's go get your luggage. It'll be in the baggage area," Uncle Ham says. He follows the signs and I follow him.

While we wait, Aunt Beulah says, "I hear you got moved up in school, that you're already in the tenth grade." She looks at me like she's figuring something out. "Mr. McPherson says you're a good student." I shrug a little, but I smile. Adults always want to talk about school.

Then she and Uncle Ham talk about how nice Mac was on the phone. Nobody mentions Mom.

As soon as we get into their car, Aunt Beulah says, "Let's stop at the store, Ham. That way Sue can pick out some food she'd like to have on hand." She turns to look at me in the back seat. "What do you like to eat, dear?"

I think about that. Home food hasn't gotten any better except for Miss Maude's desserts. Lots of canned green beans and corn, canned spaghetti, and doughy white bread.

I lean toward Aunt Beulah. "I like real tomatoes. And oranges. And I love tuna fish sandwiches and tomato soup." Then I say, "Thank you for asking, Aunt Beulah." Miss Maude would sure be proud of me.

Uncle Ham is smiling as he drives along. "Well, Beulah, I bet Sue is tired from her trip. Maybe we could pass on the store for today. How about we go straight home, and let Sue get out of that fancy dress and into some farm clothes."

Aunt Beulah gives a sigh. "All right, Ham. But we'll go tomorrow then for sure."

Aunt Beulah's long gray braids are wound around the top of her head. She holds them in place with lots of silver-colored bobby pins. When I was little, Mom used to braid my hair and wrap it in a circle like that. Maybe she learned how to do it when we stayed with Uncle Ham and Aunt Beulah that time. I decide not to ask.

The back of Uncle Ham's neck is dark, like he spends a lot of time in the sun. His thin hair sticks out over his collar. I like the way he sits up tall and straight as he drives.

After a while, he rolls down the window and sticks his arm out. That's the way Les signals. We slow down and turn left onto a small bumpy dirt road. Aunt Beulah reaches over and pats Uncle Ham on the knee. "We're almost home," she says.

I cross my fingers for good luck. August is a long way away. I look out the window and all I see is sand and big cactus plants. It's like looking at pictures in geography books. We turn a corner and pass some cows standing in a brown field. What do they eat if everything is brown here? I wonder.

We slow down even more and then turn onto what looks like a trail. It's barely wide enough for the car. We pass a bunch more sand and some dried out bushes and trees, then Uncle Ham slows down and stops.

There's a beige house right next to the car. It's kind of flat, like ranch houses I've seen in western movies. There's a wide step leading up to the porch. Off to one side, there's wire fencing. Maybe it's the turkey pen I remember from our visit back then when the turkeys pecked at me. It makes me shudder a little.

Aunt Beulah climbs out of the car, closes the heavy door behind her, and makes her way to the porch. She moves slowly in the heat. Uncle Ham holds his seat forward so I can climb out of the back. He lifts my suitcase out of the huge trunk, and I follow him and the suitcase into the dark house.

"I keep the shutters closed so the house will stay cool," Aunt Beulah announces as she turns on a table lamp. "It's something we do down here, what with the heat." She dabs at her round face with a handkerchief.

I look around. On my right, there's a wall with a lot of book-cases. To me, that's a good sign. Under the front window, there's a plain, yellow-green couch that looks like it might be hard. But right next to it, there's a big, soft chair with pink flowers that looks good for reading. The room is cool and quiet. It feels peaceful.

There's a doorway across from me that I guess leads to the rest of the house. Uncle Ham goes through that doorway and starts down a hall carrying my suitcase. "You'll be staying in the guest room," he calls to me over his shoulder. By the time I catch up, he's standing inside the bedroom. I look around.

"Wow, Uncle Ham. It's the biggest room I've ever stayed in." He laughs.

The walls are covered with dark wood. Right next to the door, there's a low chest of drawers with a big round mirror. When I sit down on the edge of the bed, I can see myself in it. "This is really great," I tell him. "Thank you."

He smiles and places my suitcase on top of the chest. "Well, I'd better go help your Aunt Beulah in the kitchen. Chances are, you'll be hungry before long." He grins and makes a funny salute. Then he closes the door behind him.

The ocean

The next morning after breakfast, Uncle Ham is sitting beside me at the little round table in the dining room. We can see Aunt Beulah standing at the sink, rinsing off our breakfast dishes. The kitchen is so close to us, it's almost part of the dining room. Uncle Ham gives me a little smile and then turns towards Aunt Beulah. "You know,

Beulah, we should go to the ocean before we go to the store." He winks at me.

Aunt Beulah stops rinsing and turns to look at Uncle Ham. "That's miles out of the way, Ham." She sounds kind of annoyed. "It'll be hot as blazes by the time we do our shopping. And Sue will be all sandy." She raises her eyebrows at Uncle Ham like he's supposed to get some kind of message.

"Well, Beulah, the child didn't come all the way down here to go to the store." I squeeze my lips together so I don't giggle out loud. I don't want Aunt Beulah mad at me.

"Oh, all right, Hamilton." She raises her silvery eyebrows again. "I suppose you'd like me to pack a lunch?"

"That would be splendid, dear." He takes a few steps to the kitchen and pats her on the shoulder.

"Tuna salad sandwiches coming up." She glances at me. "You go ahead and change, Sue."

I hurry to my super big bedroom and rummage through my suitcase until I find my new swimsuit. It's blue with white trim around the straps and down the sides. It looks like I'm on the swim team or something, which feels pretty cool. Miss Maude helped me pick it out. I pull it on and climb into a pair of navy cotton shorts and an old T-shirt. I don't know if I'm supposed to bring a towel, but I get one out of the bathroom just in case.

So far, I've mostly been in the pool at En-Joie Park and in the Susquehanna River where we swim at the Home. A long time ago, Mom said we lived near the ocean, but I was really little. I feel kind of tingly inside.

When we get in the car and Uncle Ham starts driving, they don't even talk about where we're going. I figure maybe they go here a lot. Aunt Beulah has her needlework spread out on her lap. I roll down the back window. The air is hot on my face, but I don't care. Somehow, here I am and my aunt and uncle seem okay and we're going to the ocean!

As soon as Uncle Ham stops the car and turns off the engine, I hear a big roar.

"That's the sound of the ocean," Uncle Ham yells. He's got a big grin.

I close my eyes. It sounds like a whole bunch of cars racing down a really long hill. After a few seconds, the sound goes away. I hold my breath. Then it comes back again, with a huge BOOM. Uncle Ham opens my door and I practically jump out of the car. "Oh, Uncle Ham, it's so LOUD," I yell. He nods and laughs.

We carry our lunch, a blanket, and towels as we climb up a small sandy hill. When we get to the top, I stop and stare. The blue-green ocean is so enormous, I can't see the end of it. I can't even imagine it! It's like God or somebody turned the sky upside-down and plunked it on the earth. I watch as the water runs up on the sand, then slides back. By now, I'm jumping up and down. I look at Uncle Ham, and he nods toward the roaring, waving ocean.

"Go get it, girl," he yells. "But be careful! Stay near the edge."

I pull off my shorts and T-shirt and run down the far side of the hill in my new blue swimsuit. I don't stop until I reach the dark, wet sand. I stand there and wait while the ocean swirls over my feet. Now my toes are curling beneath the bubbles. I take a deep breath and sit down on the water's edge in the wet sand.

After a few minutes, I turn around. Aunt Beulah and Uncle Ham have set things out on the side of the small sandy hill on what looks like a big, old army blanket. Aunt Beulah is putting paper plates and the sandwiches she wrapped that morning in waxed paper on the blanket. I stand up, brush the sand off my legs and run toward them.

"I love the ocean," I yell as I dance up the little hill, and they laugh and nod.

As soon as we eat, I excuse myself and dash back down the hill so I can plop down right on the edge of the water. The greenish shimmery ocean rolls in and slips back out. The swishing sounds like a lullaby. I close my eyes.

"Come on, honey, you can do it!" Mom and I were at the beach and she was calling to me. I think I was about two years old. I remember being bent over, my diapered bottom in the air, pushing a peanut in a shell in the sand with my nose. It was some kind of a race. A whole bunch of us little kids from Westport were doing this. When I got sand up my nose, I ran over to Mom on the sidelines so she could dust it off my face. Dad was there, too, I remember. He was sitting in a big green beach chair and smiling.

Before he left us for good, we spent a lot of time by the ocean. Back in Connecticut, they used to call it the shore. Mom would tell her friends, "Look at Sue-Sue. She's my little mermaid."

I open my eyes when I hear Aunt Beulah's voice call out to me over the sound of the waves. "It's time to leave for the store, Sue. Let's get ready." I make a face and stand up. Then I lean over and dig my name in the cool wet sand in really big dark sandy letters. I stare at it. Then I cross my fingers on both hands and close my eyes. "Please God, when I grow up, I want to live by the ocean. Amen."

Ronnie

The parking lot that's all around the store is full of cars. I mean, FULL. When we finally come in through the front doors, we have to wind our way through lines of people who are trying to check out. I follow Aunt Beulah, who is walking fast like she's on a mission.

We go through aisle after aisle filled with cereal boxes and jars of pickles and bottles of ketchup and more cans of Campbell's soup than I've ever seen in one place. The fresh vegetables fill up the whole length of one wall. I guess they have huge crowded stores like this in the town of Binghamton, but then Home kids only get to buy food in little shops like the one where I got the powdered sugar for Miss Maude.

I push the cart along behind Aunt Beulah and try to keep up. She puts cans of sauces and fancy ingredients I've never heard of in the basket. We spend a lot of time picking out big red tomatoes and some fancy looking lettuce. Uncle Ham goes along beside her, but he doesn't pay much attention. Finally, she lets us know she's finished shopping, and we find a place in line.

When it's our turn to check out, a man shows up and begins to stack our groceries into big brown paper bags. Aunt Beulah pokes Uncle Ham in the arm and whispers something to him. Uncle Ham just nods as he takes some more soup cans out of our cart.

Then Aunt Beulah calls out, "Ronnie! How nice to see you." She sounds excited. I look around to see who she's talking to. Her eyes are on the guy packing our stuff. He looks older than high school, like maybe he's in college. He smiles and nods hello as he piles our food in the bags.

"How are you?" Beulah asks. "And how was this last semester?"

"Oh, pretty good, Mrs. Minnerly."

He looks over at us and smiles again. His eyes are the color of old jeans, and his glasses are the same dull color as his face. He's tall, but he's all kind of washed out looking, kind of beige, like he's never out in the sun. As he packs, he keeps reaching up to smooth his hair. I can tell he puts stuff on it to hold it down. He's gentle with the tomatoes.

Aunt Beulah squeezes my shoulder. "Ronnie, this is our niece. Her name is Sue. I believe I've mentioned her." Ronnie grins at me and nods again. Aunt Beulah continues. "Sue's spending the whole summer with us." She gives my shoulder another little squeeze and looks at me like she's seeing my face for the first time. "Ronnie is going to college in Gainesville where he's studying to be an archi-tect." She sounds so proud, like he's her son.

Ronnie finishes packing and wipes his hands off on his apron. He takes a long look at my face. Then he stares at the rest of me. I'm kind of getting used to being checked out by the boys at school, but this is different, like he's prying.

I take a quick look down to see what he sees. Long sandy legs and skinny feet. Holes in the toes of my sneakers. Blue cotton shorts, new but sandy, and a big, loose T-shirt. I can't see my hair, but I figure it's pretty much a mess after our time at the beach. Miss Maude gave me a perm before I left for the summer, so I know it's way too curly.

Ronnie holds out his hand. I look at Aunt Beulah to see if I'm supposed to shake with him, but she's busy counting out dollar bills on the counter. When I put my hand out, he takes it and hangs on. I feel my face turn red. After a while, he says, "Pleased to meet you," and lets go.

I glance at Uncle Ham, who is over by the magazine rack. Aunt Beulah calls out to him, "Ham? Can you come help with the groceries? We're ready to leave."

Ronnie gets behind our cart and pushes it toward the door. Soon we're going through the jammed up parking lot. I speed up so I'm ahead of him but he hurries with the cart and catches up.

"Just get to Fort Lauderdale?" he asks. The cart bumps along in front of him.

"Yesterday."

"Florida's nice. I bet you're gonna like it here."

I nod to be polite, but I don't look at him. Who is this guy, and why is he paying so much attention to me? Uncle Ham unlocks the car and lets me in on his side, while Ronnie puts the groceries in the trunk. I slide over behind Beulah's seat and close my eyes.

When Aunt Beulah doesn't get in the car after I hear the trunk slam shut, I open my eyes. She's still in the parking lot, talking to Ronnie. It's so hot in the car, I wind my window down part way. That's when I hear her say, "Well, what do you think?" I watch his hand come up until it's level with the window. Then he gives her a big thumbs-up sign. Aunt Beulah laughs. I look at Uncle Ham to see what he thinks, but he's staring out the driver's side window.

Ronnie helps Aunt Beulah take her place in the front seat and closes her door. She's humming. Uncle Ham starts the car. I take a quick look outside. Ronnie is wiping his hands on his apron and staring at me. I look away.

Aunt Beulah

In the next week, I get all the way through two new Nancy Drew stories. Then I read *The Secret Garden* again. I already read it in the little library next to Mac's office, but it's such a good story, I don't mind reading it again. Plus, it feels so good to curl up in the living room in the soft chair with the pink flowers.

When it's cool enough, I walk barefoot around the farm. Most days, though, the sandy soil is too hot. Boy, it's a good thing I don't live in this heat all the time.

In the late afternoons when I'm sitting in my favorite flowered chair, I can see Aunt Beulah across the room in the kitchen making dinner. She sure moves faster in there than anywhere else. Sometimes she hums. Her face gets shiny, I guess because it's pretty hot in there with the stove on. I like the way her silver braids stay wound around the top of her head and little strands of hair curl beside her ears.

One afternoon, I get the idea of helping her make dinner. Maybe that would be good and we'd get to know each other. Well, at least a little.

I put my book on the small round wooden table that's next to my reading chair and wander over toward the kitchen door. She's singing to herself, so I don't want to interrupt. But then, standing and watching doesn't feel right either. So I knock just a little on the door frame, like it was the front door to the house.

"Hi, Aunt Beulah? Can I help with something?"

She swings around and stares at me.

"Oh my goodness, Sue, you surprised me. I forgot you were here." Saying that makes her cheeks get red, like she's embarrassed. She rubs her hands on her pretty ruffled apron as she glances around the room. She's looking for something for me to do, I bet. Right away, she picks up a green pepper.

"Would you mind cutting this into little pieces for me?" she asks. "I'd like to add it to the meatloaf I'm making for supper." She looks at me with a frown. "I hope you like meatloaf."

"Oh, sure, I like meatloaf." Sometimes I do anyway.

I take the pepper and cross over to the kitchen sink. There's a small wooden cutting board on the counter right next to it. Aunt Beulah pulls open a drawer and takes out a small paring knife.

"Here, use this."

We don't ever get to help make dinner at the Home. I hope I don't make a mess of this. I begin to chop part of the pepper into really small pieces. That's how Mom used to do it.

I can feel Aunt Beulah watching me. "Is this okay?" I ask her.

"Oh my, yes. That's just fine." She smiles and turns back to the meatloaf and pours some bread crumbs in it. I keep chopping.

"I've been thinking about your mom," she says. I freeze up a little and keep my eyes down. We chop and mix for a while in silence. "How's she doing, Sue?" I look out of the corner of my eye. Beulah is keeping her eyes down too as she mixes the meatloaf in the bowl.

"She's okay. I guess." Chop, dice, slice off another piece of pepper. "She got married, you know."

"Oh yes," Aunt Beulah says. She has a funny smile in her voice. "His name is Lester, is that right?"

"Uh huh." I don't say any more.

"Sue, could you get me an egg? I've got meatloaf all over my fingers." She holds them up so I can see.

I walk behind her to the big white refrigerator. She keeps the eggs in a little plastic holder that sits in the door. I take one out.

When I turn around, Aunt Beulah looks sad, tired, almost worn out. She rubs the back of her hand across her forehead.

"I remember when you and your mom were here. That was so many years ago." She shakes her head. "It was so hard for her when your dad left." She looks at me, stares into my eyes. "It was hard on you, too, I know."

I hand her the egg and go back to chopping the pepper.

"Do you miss living with her Sue?"

Aunt Beulah's voice is soft now, the softest I've ever heard from her. I look over at her. She's staring out the kitchen window like she's remembering. She turns back to me.

"I'm sorry, Sue. I shouldn't be intruding in your business."

She cracks the eggshell and drops the raw egg into the meatloaf mixture. I look down at the little chopped up bits of pepper. I'm not sure what to say. Or how to explain anything. Or even if I should try.

"It didn't work," I tell her. I take a deep breath. "I did go home for a while back when I was twelve, but Mom was still . . . upset." My head feels scrambled.

"Well." Aunt Beulah's voice is strong. "It seems like you're doing okay at the Home. Do you like it there?"

I wipe the edge of the knife on a dishcloth that's lying on the counter while I think about that.

"I like Miss Maude a lot. And Mac. And I have some friends there now. It was hard before, but yeah, I guess it's all right."

She comes over to me and picks up the small cutting board with the tiny green pepper pieces on it.

"Well, I hope you like it here, Sue. Maybe you'll want to stay down here with us, at least for a while. After all, we are your family." She gives me a wide smile, but it doesn't look real.

By the time I turn toward her, she's back at the meatloaf folding in the pepper pieces.

Time passes

Ronnie's here again. It's the third time in two weeks. The four of us are eating supper at the little round table. The ceiling fan makes a clicking noise as it goes around. This time Aunt Beulah baked chicken pieces with mushroom soup and broccoli. She does most of the talking. She wants to make sure I hear all about Ronnie and what a "bright future" he has. I hear about his parents, too. Ronnie leans toward me and says, "They'd like to meet you, Sue. Maybe I can take you by the house one day soon." I freeze. Boy, that sure keeps me quiet for the rest of the meal.

After dinner, Aunt Beulah tells Ronnie and me to "shoo" out of the kitchen and go have fun. Tonight, like the other nights, we walk down the driveway. We don't say much. I listen to the crickets and the bullfrogs. I make sure I keep a lot of space between us. I cross my arms.

We're maybe thirty feet from the house when Ronnie stops in the middle of the driveway.

"Sue," he says, "I know your birthday's coming up." He looks down as he starts stubbing at the ground with the toe of his shoe. "I wonder if I could take you someplace. You know. To celebrate?" I feel his eyes on me. I look away and don't say anything. After a little while, he says, "Maybe we could have a picnic at the beach. Just you and me."

I shrug and start back up the driveway toward the house. Here I am in Florida, a zillion miles away from Miss Maude and Mac, and this older guy wants to take me on a picnic for my fifteenth birthday! Boy, I know if Aunt Beulah has her way, I'll spend that whole day with him, but it just plain feels wrong. He's already twenty-three and in grad school! The boys I know are fifteen or sixteen. They're not like him. I hardly know how to act around a guy who stares at me long and hard like Ronnie does.

I stop. Oh God, what if he wants to touch me like Nan did?

I start moving again. I lower my eyes and stare at the driveway. My face feels sweaty and uncomfortable. Oh geez, I remember that time when she climbed into my bed. I lift my eyes and walk faster. Don't think about that, I tell myself. Just keep going.

I stride along and fuss over this in my head. I know Aunt Beulah would be crazy-happy if Ronnie and I had a 'date' or something. But what about Uncle Ham? He's so quiet when Ronnie comes over for dinner, it's like he's not really in the room. I wish I could figure out what he thinks of Ronnie. If I say no to going out with him, will Uncle Ham take my side?

Finally, I get to the front porch and turn around. Ronnie is so close behind me, I quick reach for the doorknob.

"Thank you for asking," I tell him. Even now, I'm trying to be polite. "I'll think about it."

I slip inside and quick shut the door behind me. I plunk down in my flowered chair in the dark. This farm in Florida doesn't feel like a safe place right now. It makes me think about what scared me when Mom and I came here such a long time ago.

I was four years old. Mom and I were out in the yard when, all of a sudden, the sky turned dark and a wild storm hit with a huge bang and lightning. Right away, Mom grabbed me and held on with both hands. She yelled, but the wind was so loud I couldn't hear what she said. The rain on my face felt like needles. Mom whipped me around so we were facing Uncle Ham's house. She wrapped her arms around me and started to pull me toward the front door. There was so much wind, I could hardly breathe. I thought maybe this was the end of the world, like that Sunday school teacher said would happen.

The wind and rain kept pushing us farther away from the house. The storm was so loud, it was like it was screaming. Mom leaned over me and pointed to a huge old tree. Some of its branches were already broken and on the ground. She held on to me and pressed her mouth against my ear. "We'll go hang on to the tree," she yelled. Just then, a silver pail flew by and she threw her arm up to shield us. When the pail smashed into her arm, I started to cry.

As soon as we reached the tree, she pressed against me so I was flat against the trunk. "Keep your head down, Sue-Sue," she hollered. "And hang on." I saw blood and scratches on her arms, but she didn't let go.

When the wind began to slow down, Mom grabbed my hand and pulled me across the yard and into the house. As soon as we got to the living room, she picked me up and laid me down on the couch. She didn't even take off my wet sandy dress and my messed up sandals. She pulled a blanket up over me and tucked me in. Then she sat on the edge of the couch and smoothed my wet hair out of my eyes. "It's okay, honey. It's all over now." She said this over and over. I remember crying a lot before I finally fell asleep.

I get up from my flowered chair and go through the dark living room to my bedroom. Ronnie doesn't make Florida feel any safer now than it did years ago during that storm. And Beulah doesn't help. I close the bedroom door and turn on the little lamp that's on my dresser. Plunking down on the edge of the bed, I see a giant cockroach crawling across the floor. Down here, they call them palmetto bugs, but I know it's a plain old cockroach. I watch it slide inside a crack in the wall. I feel like that bug, like I need to find a hole in the wall and crawl in it.

I squish my pillow so it's just right, turn out the light, and close my eyes. I don't want to think about my birthday anymore. Or about having a bunch more weeks in Florida. Or about Ronnie.

Birthday girl

I'm *steaming*. It's my birthday and I'm stuck in Ronnie's car and he's driving me to the beach! Aunt Beulah said I had to go. I'm sitting as close as I can to the door. I slouch down, cross my arms, and stare out the window.

As soon as he stops, I climb out and hurry up over the sand dune and down to the ocean. He can carry the lunch basket and all the rest of the stuff. I don't care.

There are long rows of big black boulders going out into the sea at each end of the beach. I think they're called jetties. The sand is so clean and white, it's like a movie. I look around. There's a family not too far away. That's good. I don't feel safe alone with him.

Standing by the edge of the ocean, I watch Ronnie up on the sand dune spreading out the blanket. He likes things neat and tidy. I try to relax. After all, it *is* my birthday and I'm at the ocean. I walk back up the dune and sit down on the edge of the blanket. I don't let myself get comfortable.

Ronnie plops down beside me but he doesn't say much. Just polite stuff.

"Is this spot okay?"

"Uh huh."

"Isn't the beach pretty?"

"Yes."

"Do you want a soda?"

"No, thank you."

As soon as he leans close to me and starts rubbing my arm, I jump up and walk fast back down to the ocean.

He catches up with me. We don't say anything. I turn around so I can I walk backward on the wet sand. That way I don't have to look at him. I stare at our footprints. His are big and deep, mine are skinny and light, like I'm barely touching the ground.

"Hey, let's go swimming," he announces. I stop. I look out at the sea and think about when I first learned to swim. Suddenly, I want to have water all around me.

"Okay," I yell. "Let's go!"

I quick strip down to my bathing suit and run into the waves. I do all this really fast. Ronnie is behind me hopping on one foot as he pulls off his shoe.

"Wait up, Sue," he yells. "I'm supposed to look out for you."

The ocean water is cool on my skin. It helps me calm down. I keep my eye on the horizon like Mom always told me to and start swimming, pumping my arms and kicking my feet.

It doesn't take long for Ronnie to catch up. Almost out of breath, I flip onto my back and let the salt water hold me up. Now Ronnie's right beside me treading water. I close my eyes so I can feel like I'm alone.

"Hey, Sue. Let's go climb on the rocks." I open my eyes a little. He's swimming toward the jetty.

The rocks look almost as tall as I am. I watch Ronnie climb up and find a flat place to sit. After a while I get tired of treading water, so I climb up, too. I do it by myself. We sit in silence and watch the ocean splash on the rocks around us. After a while, I close my eyes and lean back in the warm sun. That's when I feel his arms go all around me.

"Stop it! Just stop it!" I yell. I push him away hard and start clambering down to the water. The rock edges scratch my arms and legs.

"Sue, come on, I want us to be friends!" He's up on a rock behind me hollering and he sounds mad.

Friends? Baloney. I jump off the lowest rock I can find and swim hard toward the shore. Right away I hear a splash behind me.

I pump my arms and kick hard, but he's so strong he's already beside me. As soon as my feet touch bottom, I push through the water and run up on the sand. When I stop to get my breath, he tries to grab me. I pull away and grab my shorts and T-shirt. My shirt starts to rip when I stick my arms in.

Ronnie reaches down and yanks up his slacks. "Sue, I'm sorry. I don't mean to upset you." He's kind of yelling, breathing hard. "It's just that I really like you. And damn it, I want you to like me back." We stand there, wet and sandy, with him scowling and with me crying and really mad. That's when he stuffs his hand in one of his pants pockets. He pulls out a small white box and slaps it in my hand.

"Happy birthday, Sue." He sounds angry and sad.

Before I know what I'm doing, I lift the lid on the box. Inside is a heart on a silver chain. It's covered with little baby diamonds that flash and twinkle in the sunlight. I turn and run for the car.

Missing Miss Maude

"Oh Miss Maude," I whisper. I'm curled up in my bed in the dark on my birthday night. "I miss you a lot. And I miss Mac. And Donna." When I think about saying that I miss Mom too, the tears start.

Sometimes I wish I knew how to call Miss Maude on my aunt and uncle's phone. I've never made a long-distance call before. I don't want to ask anybody here how to do that. Plus it would cost them money. And what if she doesn't have a solution for me. And besides, I'm fifteen now and should be able to figure this out, I guess.

I close my eyes and think about Miss Maude's curly gray-white hair and her shiny blue eyes. It's sort of silly, but she makes me think of Mrs. Santa Claus. I bet right now she's sitting in the living room in her favorite big brown chair with her pack of Kool cigarettes on the table right next to her.

I turn my pillow over and put my cheek down on the cool side. Like most nights, crickets and bullfrogs make singing noises outside my window. I whisper to Miss Maude, like she's here.

"Aunt Beulah picked out a boyfriend for me." I stew about that for a minute.

"I know they want me to like him, but I don't." I pull the top sheet up to my chin and think about how he's always trying to touch me. It makes me close my eyes and scrunch up my face.

"He's going to school to be an architect. Aunt Beulah says he'll have a good job later on." I stop and think about the heart necklace he gave me. "I guess he likes me a lot."

I close my eyes tight and pretend Miss Maude is sitting on the edge of my bed listening to me. I can almost feel her there. I smooth the sheets and think about what I need to say.

"This guy Ronnie wants to be my boyfriend, but it's not right. For one thing, it gives me the creeps, the way he stares at me. He's twenty-three, and that feels like he's too old. I keep telling Aunt Beulah I don't want him for a boyfriend, but she laughs." Silence. "I wish you were here."

It's muggy and I kick off the covers.

"Oh. Guess what. Something good happened." I feel the knot in my stomach start to melt. "I made a friend. I think so anyway. His name is Charles. He's sixteen. He had polio when he was little, and he has to use special crutches when he walks. My aunt and uncle took me to visit his family, and Charles and I got to talk and listen to records. He's really smart. And he didn't stare at me weird or want to rub my arms or anything. Even Uncle Ham says he thinks Charles would make a good friend. So maybe I don't need to worry about Ronnie so much."

I close my eyes.

Help from a friend

It's the beginning of August before we go to Charles's house again. As my aunt and uncle and Charles's parents begin to settle in at the bridge table, Charles calls over to me, "Let's go out on the screened porch." I nod and wait while he shifts around in his chair and finally gets himself upright and on his crutches. It takes some time.

I watch him get settled on one side of the glider, then I start toward an old wicker chair on the other side of the porch. "Wait a minute," Charles calls as he scrunches over to make room for me. "We can talk better here." He pats the cushion. Then he leans his crutches against the wall beside him.

"Who's that guy your aunt talks about?" he asks as I sit down. Before long, I'm telling Charles about Ronnie, how he hangs around all the time and how he gave me a sparkly necklace for my birthday. I don't say much about him touching me.

We rock back and forth on the glider.

After a while, Charles says, "You've had some pretty weird stuff going on with this Ronnie guy this summer." We rock for a minute. "How about if you had something really fun to remember when you get back to the Home?"

I stare at him. I don't know what to expect. As we rock slowly back and forth, Charles continues. "Sue, I'm not after you like Ronnie is. Don't worry." He's looking at the floor.

Then he looks at me. "I know you love the ocean. But I bet you've never seen it from way up high." He shifts around a little bit on the glider. "So I'm thinking, there's a restaurant my parents go to. It's on the top floor of a hotel, and if you and I went there, we could look right down at the ocean while we eat."

I look at what's in his eyes. I want to be sure he wants to be my friend, and nothing more. "Where is this place?"

"My folks say they'll take us there and bring us back." I roll my eyes. "Don't worry. They're not going to have dinner with us. They figure we have stuff to talk about, being teens and all." We laugh a little.

"So. How soon do you go back?"

"I'm not sure. I mean, I'm supposed to go on August 25th, just before school starts. But Aunt Beulah has my plane ticket, so I don't really know . . . ."

I lower my head and close my eyes and think about stuff.

Some nights, I stay awake and listen to Aunt Beulah and Ronnie talking in the kitchen. They keep dreaming up ways to get me to stay in Florida. One time, she and Uncle Ham even took me over to Ronnie's house to meet his parents. His mom gave me a hankie. It had my name on it.

"I embroidered it for you," she told me.

I know Ronnie is going back to college in September, but I also know, sure as I have a little heart-shaped necklace on my dresser, that his parents want me to stay in Florida and be Ronnie's girlfriend. Or maybe more.

Charles gives me a nudge.

"Sue, what's up?" he asks. "You seem really sad. Is it about going to this fancy place? I mean, we don't have to. I thought you'd get a kick out of it."

I shake my head. "That's not it. It's other stuff."

I think about things some more. I need to talk to someone. I need to talk to Charles.

"Look, I know you're not like Ronnie. So how about we go to this place and just have fun? And we'll talk about stuff. And look at the ocean."

I watch his face. It always looks strong and determined. It's thin, and what my mom would call angular. He's got a great grin now that I've said I'll go, and he's *not* looking at me the way Ronnie does.

"I'm glad you're my friend, Charles."

A week later, his parents pick me up at the farm. Charles and I sit in the back seat, and his mom and dad pretend to be our drivers, like we're in a limousine.

His mom turns and looks at us in the back. "Sue! You look so pretty in that dress," she tells me. I'm wearing my yellow dress with the green sash. It's the first time since the plane ride.

Charles has on a suit and a spiffy tie covered with little silver stars.

"What a neat tie!" I tell him.

"I'm going to call it Sue's tie," he tells me, looking down at it. "I don't like to wear one very much." His mom laughs.

They drive us all the way to Miami to the Fontainebleau Hotel. His dad drives into the garage below the hotel. "There's an elevator here so you guys won't have to walk all the way up the front steps of the hotel."

As we climb out and wave good-bye, the elevator arrives, as if on cue. Charles presses the top button. It says "Restaurant."

When the elevator doors slide open, we're right inside the restaurant. Boy, is it fancy. There are lots of glass chandeliers and white tablecloths and flowers on the tables. Charles gives his name to a dark-haired, dark-skinned young waiter, who checks us off on a list of names and leads us across the room to a table next to a window. When the waiter pulls out my chair, I feel like I'm a princess in a story. After Charles is seated, the waiter picks up Charles's crutches from the floor. He's very careful with them.

"May I check these in the coatroom for you sir, until you are ready to leave?"

Charles nods. "Yes, thank you."

Wow!

The sun is starting to sink now. We can see people walking along on the sand as waves come rolling in. While we eat really good fish and a big salad, Charles and I talk about school. He likes it as much as I do, except he's crazy about math. He tells me how he hates his crutches and how kids don't like to look at him. I tell him about Miss Maude and Mac and how great they are. And then I talk about Mrs. Labee and how the girls used to beat me up.

Finally, by the time dessert comes, I'm talking about Ronnie.

"He's driving me crazy," I tell Charles. "And I'm scared Aunt Beulah and Uncle Ham won't let me leave. I think they want me to stay here to be with him." When I start to sniffle, Charles signals the waiter.

"Would you bring my friend a Shirley Temple, please?" he asks. "She needs something to help calm her nerves." Now I'm laughing. Even the waiter is smiling.

"Certainly, sir," he says with a small bow.

"You know, Sue, maybe your best chance at getting rid of all this stuff with Ronnie is to have a really good talk with your uncle." Charles looks serious.

"But Aunt Beulah's the one behind this," I tell him.

"I know." There's a pause. I can tell he's really thinking about this. "But your uncle really cares about you. I think he'll do the right thing. But you have to tell him what that is."

A talk with Uncle Ham

For a few days, I stew about what to say and how to say it. Then one night, when Aunt Beulah goes back to the kitchen to clean up after dinner, Uncle Ham stands up and begins to move toward the front porch. He does this a lot after dinner. I'm by myself in the living room. I watch him through the window as he settles down in his favorite rocker. He lights a Marlboro and leans back.

It's not completely dark out yet. I think about how important this is, how much getting away from Ronnie means to me. And about how much I'm learning to care about my life. I whisper, "Okay, kiddo, here we go," and cross my fingers for luck.

I slip outside and sit down at the top of the porch steps. I turn sideways a little and lean back against the rail post. This way, I can see Uncle Ham out of the corner of my eye, but I don't have to look right at him.

I've learned a few things about my uncle. For one thing, he likes to keep Aunt Beulah happy. He doesn't like it when she gets upset and starts carrying on about stuff. He also likes sitting alone by himself in the evening, looking out at the night sky, and listening to the crickets. Sometimes he walks down the driveway, humming. I've also figured out that he doesn't really like Ronnie that much. I guess he thinks Ronnie's pretty smart and a "good catch" as Aunt Beulah would say, but I don't think he likes being around him. Sometimes he makes an excuse to leave the room when Ronnie comes over to visit. I think maybe he doesn't want Ronnie to . . . I stop. It's too scary.

I've learned, too, that he cares about my mom. Once he told me he was sorry she was having such a hard time. Uncle Ham doesn't like it that my dad, who's a "rich son-of-a-gun," doesn't give her enough money to get along on. Uncle Ham knows about the time Mom worked in a factory and got sick. "Peg's not cut out for that sort of life," he said. He sounded sad. "Is she still pretty?" he asked me once. I nodded yes, and he smiled as though remembering what my mom looked like when she was a young girl. He told me about the time she put lemon juice on her face and sat outside half the night during a full moon because a girlfriend told her that would get rid of her freckles.

Through the little window to the kitchen, I can see Aunt Beulah scraping and rinsing dishes and putting them in the dishpan. She has the radio on low. I don't think she can hear us, but I want to be careful.

"Good supper, huh," I say to Uncle Ham.

"Yeah, Beulah does a nice job in the kitchen," he answers. I listen to the creak of his chair. He's rocking back and forth in a slow, comfortable way.

"Uncle Ham?" I keep my voice quiet, like I'm just talking about supper or the crickets. "When am I going back to Binghamton?"

The creaking stops. "Do you want to go back to the Home, Sue?"

I think about that. "Well, it's not my favorite place in the world. But Mom's nearby. And Mac and Miss Maude are really nice. And all my stuff is at the Home now. I really like my school, too."

In my head, I hear Miss Maude tell me, "You're rambling, Sue."

I sit up straight. "Yes, Uncle Ham, I want to go back."

I'm afraid as I say it out loud like that. I don't want to hurt him. So I add, "But I'll miss you and Aunt Beulah, that's for sure. You've been really good to me, bringing me down here and everything."

The rocker starts creaking again.

"You know, Sue, your Aunt Beulah wants you to have a good life. She doesn't want to send you back to that factory town, as she calls it."

Out of the corner of my eye, I watch him stare into the night. Smoke from his cigarette curls up toward the porch roof. After a while, he continues.

"She thinks you'd be better off down here. You could finish high school and then, if all goes well, maybe you and your young man could get married."

I'm so shocked, I stand up. I keep my eyes forward like Uncle Ham and make my voice strong. "Uncle Ham, I don't love Ronnie. I don't even like him. He's too old. And he's creepy." I turn to face my uncle. "I don't want to stay here." When he doesn't say anything, I announce, "I don't want to marry Ronnie. I just want to go home."

"Sue, honey, you're young and you don't understand a lot of things. We want what's best for you." His voice is slow and gentle, but what he's saying scares me.

"Well, I want to go back. That's all there is to it." Out of nowhere, I start to cry. Hurt and embarrassed, I stand there in the dark. The only other people who can help me are thousands of miles away.

"We'll see," is all he says. Then he stubs out his cigarette and walks into the house.

The ticket

Days pass. It feels like forever. I'm supposed to be on a plane in less than a week. I wander around the little farm with my fingers crossed for luck. I say good-bye to the turkeys, good-bye to the bullfrogs and the crickets, and good-bye to the sand that's everywhere. I want to go to the ocean one more time, but I'm afraid to ask. It might seem like I'm giving in. "Sue will stay here," Aunt Beulah will think, "to be near the ocean." So I don't say anything.

I spend a lot of time in my room reading and listening to the radio. I mope around. Even though I love tuna sandwiches, one day I leave half of one uneaten on the plate. Maybe Aunt Beulah will figure out I'm upset. Or sick. Or something. I pack my suitcase and leave it propped on top of the bureau. I want her to see it whenever she looks in my room. Each day, I take out only what I'm going to wear. I try every way I can think of to show them I want to leave. I want them to figure out that making me stay in Florida won't work.

Tomorrow is the day, but Aunt Beulah still has the ticket. Each night, I've asked God to make sure the plane doesn't take off without me. It's all so scary, I feel like I'm going to throw up.

While I try to figure out what to do, I sit on my bed and stare at a boring magazine about farm life. Everything in it looks boring. Outside, the wind is blowing so hard, the treetops are shaking. The air is damp and stirred up. It feels like a storm is coming, like when I was here before when I was little.

Out of the corner of my eye, I see Uncle Ham come and stand in the doorway. I look over at him. We stare at each other the way kids do sometimes when there's reason to be careful.

When he slides a white envelope out of his shirt pocket, my heart starts to pump really hard. He takes a few steps so he's right beside my suitcase and sets the envelope on top of it. He kind of nods his head a little and steps back into the doorway.

"You're going back." His voice is quiet and sort of flat. He looks over at the envelope. "Your ticket's in there. We leave for the airport after breakfast."

We have the same color eyes. I noticed it before, but now it's almost like looking into my own eyes. I'm leaving my aunt and uncle, but I'm going back to Miss Maude and Mac. I'll be a sophomore at North High. Maybe a cute boy will ask me to a dance. Maybe I'll get an A in French. Then I think about Charles. I wish I could tell him I got the ticket.

"Thank you, Uncle Ham. This means a lot to me."

He nods. "I hope it wasn't all bad down here."

I am crying now, but I'm smiling, too. "It was great. I'm glad I got to know you. I'm glad you're my uncle."

FITTING IN

Buying my first Pall Malls

As soon as I find my seat, I curl up and close my eyes. I'm so happy to just be in this airplane and not think about Ronnie or Florida or anything.

I'm barely awake when my plane lands in Binghamton. I take a good look around the waiting area, which seems really small compared to the airport in Miami, but Mac isn't here yet. I scramble around in my purse until I find a quarter. On the far side of the room behind the rows of chairs, I see one of those vending machines that has different kinds of cigarettes. Smoking makes Mom and Miss Maude and Uncle Ham feel calm, and I sure as hell want to feel like that.

I drop in my quarter, push the button, and there in the tray at the bottom lands a pack of Pall Malls. I pull the little red strip that opens the wrapper and tap the pack on the edge of my hand the way Uncle Ham does. I cough a lot, but I get one going. And I inhale right from the start. As soon as I smoke the first one, I rush into a stall in the ladies room and throw up. By the time I've smoked three, one after the other, I'm sort of used to feeling sea-sick.

I picked Pall Malls because they're Mom's brand. No filters for me. I want to feel tobacco on my lips, like Mom does. I love the way she picks a piece off the end of her tongue while she's talking, or before she takes a sip from her jelly glass. She simply removes it like it's in the way. She's the most glamorous smoker I know.

Miss Maude is different. As soon as she lights up, there's a huge blue cloud over her head. She puffs quickly, holding her cigarette with her thumb and first finger. She makes it look like it's a not-nice thing. And Miss Maude doesn't inhale. I think that's really strange. I mean, why smoke if you don't inhale? But she seems to be happy putting the little white stick between her red lips and puffing out, not in. I think about asking her why she doesn't inhale, but maybe it wouldn't be polite.

Uncle Ham, on the other hand, smokes like the guy in those cigarette ads who wears the patch over his eye. He even looks a little like him, the way he leans back in his chair and lets his cigarette dangle by his side. He holds it between his first and second fingers, low down and close to his palm. Sometimes he even cups his hand around it. If he's talking, he pauses when he takes a puff. His tan hand brings the cigarette to his lips and he takes a long pull. Then he leans back and blows smoke rings, which he usually directs toward the porch ceiling since Aunt Beulah doesn't want his "smelly tobacco" inside. After the smoke rings disappear, he'd finish his sentence. It made for some long pauses, but I sure liked to watch him.

By the time Mac finds me, I have my pack of Pall Malls tucked away in a corner of my purse and only a little bit of throw-up on my skirt. Mac hugs me, then looks at me like he can smell what's going on, but he doesn't say anything. Neither does Miss Maude. As soon as Mac drops me at the cottage, she gives me a big hug and asks me to tell her all about my trip. I know we'll talk about Florida on and off for months while I figure out the second half of tenth grade at North High.

Things unsaid

"When did you start these?"

We're sitting at the same little kitchen table Mom's had for years now. She's pointing to the pack of Pall Malls in my hand. Her voice is rough, kind of distant. She's got her jelly glass close by. I didn't want to come by the duplex after school, but she insisted. "It's been too long," she told me. "And besides, we need to have a good place to talk about your summer in Florida."

"I bought them when I got back," I tell her. I don't mention buying them right away at the airport or wanting to get calm, whatever that feels like.

She blows smoke toward the ceiling. I take a Pall Mall out of my pack and reach for the book of matches on the table.

"Does Ham still smoke?" she asks me.

"Uh huh." I light my cigarette and inhale. "Marlboros," I tell her.

I've been here about an hour now. We've talked a lot about Uncle Ham and Aunt Beulah, about their little ranch, about the tan house, about the ocean, even some about Ronnie. Not about me. I look around for a clock, but I don't see one. My bus leaves the bus stop out front at 4:40. I don't want to miss it. That gets me back to the Home right around supper time.

Mom gets up, leans on the table for a second, and then walks over to the cupboard. Time for another drink, I figure. I just hope we don't end up in a fight.

She slides the brown bottle—I know now it's a pint of rye—off the bottom shelf and unscrews the top.

"So you didn't want to stay down there? I mean, with your aunt and uncle?"

I watch her pour an inch of rye into the glass.

"Not really," I tell her. "I didn't like that guy that Beulah wanted to fix me up with. Ronnie." I inhale. "He wasn't right for me. A nice guy, I guess, but not somebody I wanted to . . . be my boyfriend." I almost say marry, but that feels like I'm going too far.

"I miss Ham, you know?" Mom turns to face me, holding her glass. There are tears drifting down her cheeks. "I miss having a family."

I nod. Boy, so do I.

"He said a lot of nice things about you, Mom. You know that story about putting lemon juice on your freckles? Well, he told me about that."

We smile now, on a topic that brings a softness to this rough time.

Mom sits across from me, twirling her glass around like she's thinking. She's almost entirely gray now, her short hair curled like she's had a perm. She's in her fifties, I figure, since she was thirty-six when I came along. She has on a plain dark skirt, like always, and a sweater with the sleeves pushed up to her elbows. I mostly think of her as tan, but now it's a faded sort of tan, like you have after summer is long gone. My hands and wrists are thin like hers, I realize.

"Did you talk about my life?" she asks. I watch her looking around the room at the old-fashioned kitchen, the worn yellow counter tops, the faded linoleum floor. "Did they ask about how I get through the day?" She holds her glass up and laughs a little.

I shake my head.

"Hey, Mom," I say. I want to change the topic. "I remember that hurricane, you know? The one we were in when you and I were down there? I was only four, right, Mom?"

She smiles at me. Her eyes, for the moment, are clear and her focus is on me, on us. "Oh, Sue-Sue, that was such a scary time. Do you remember us hanging on to that tree?"

"I sure do," I tell her, and take another drag on my Pall Mall. Mom looks down at the table.

"Well, Sue-Sue, I'm glad you decided to come . . . back."

I know she was about to say come home, but I'm not at home. I'm at *the* Home. We don't talk much about that.

She looks across the table at me.

"What grade are you in now?" she asks.

"Tenth. They put me in the second half. I'll be a junior when the next semester starts in the winter."

She nods. I've told her what grade I'm in before, but I no longer expect her to remember.

"Was it good to get back here? Back to . . . Miss Maude?"

Her question surprises me. We hardly ever talk about her.

"Yeah, I guess. But sometimes I kind of feel like I'm stuck in the wrong place, you know?"

She stands abruptly and turns away, almost knocking the little table over. Now I've done it.

"Hey, Mom, it's getting late." I say it fast, like I'm in a hurry. "Gotta get ready for my bus."

I know she and I can't talk about a lot of things, and Miss Maude and the Home are high on that list.

She keeps her back to me, but she nods. She knows I need to go. I guess there's not much else I can say about the summer, about my aunt and uncle not wanting me to come back to this.

I pick up my book bag and pull my cardigan off the back of the chair. "Let's meet in town next week. At the counter at Woolworths, like usual." I watch her back relax just a little.

"Sure, honey," she says turning toward me. "Whatever you say."

Who cares

"Why on earth did you do it, Sue?"

Miss Maude is fuming. She's sitting across from me in the living room smoking one of her Kools. It's almost dark out. I can hear the girls downstairs cleaning up after supper.

"All the kids here like her. I thought, maybe, if I were Joy's friend . . . ."

I look away. I miss Donna a lot and Miss Maude knows it. I'm glad Donna and Ellen got to go home during the summer, but it's so lonely here without her. Maybe it was crazy trying to be friends with Joy, but I need someone my age to talk to.

"You know better, Sue. Besides, you could have gotten in serious trouble."

I look up surprised. How could I get in serious trouble for skipping school?

"It wasn't 'serious trouble.' And besides it really bugs me that Mac doesn't even believe it was my idea. How come he blames Joy?"

"Well, wouldn't you?" Miss Maude shakes her head. "For heaven's sake, you've never done anything like this before. On the other hand, Joy does this all the time." She looks at me like I'm thick.

"When North High called to say you weren't there, and that Joy wasn't there either, it scared me half to death. I didn't know what to expect."

She takes a puff on her cigarette and right away blows the smoke up toward the ceiling. Boy, I wish I could have one.

"The next thing I know, I see you and Joy climbing out of the back of a police car, for God's sake." Her voice is loud, frustrated. "So, look how your bright idea to skip school turned out, young lady."

She shakes her head again. "I truly do not understand what you were thinking."

I stand and walk to the window.

I disappointed her. I made her worry. That makes me feel like I'm bad inside.

"It was my idea, Miss Maude. And I'm sorry."

"For heaven's sake, Sue, you are an honor student. You love school. This is simply not like you."

Silence.

"How did this whole thing get started?" Her voice is calmer now.

I turn toward her.

"Joy and I were walking to the bus stop yesterday when I got the idea. It was a really nice day. And I thought, maybe if we hung out together, you know, talked about stuff, maybe we could be friends."

I look away and stare out the window.

When I think of Joy, I think of bright colors and loud music. She's always at the center of things. While I'm studying, she's giggling on the phone or singing along with the radio. One night I asked her why she skipped school so much. "It's sooooo boring," she said. "A waste of my time." Then she asked me how I liked the color of her new lipstick. "I got it at Woolworths." She wiggled her fingers. "Five-finger discount."

"Sue?" Miss Maude is next to me now, shaking my shoulder.

I turn toward her.

"What's wrong, dear?"

"I don't know." Tears start to come. Miss Maude leads me back to the couch and we sit down.

"Ever since you got back from Florida, you've been out of sorts." She watches me. "You look like things don't 'fit' anymore."

I nod. "That's how I feel."

She fusses with her open pack of cigarettes. "But good things have been happening," she reminds me. "What about that sorority . . . ."

"Tau Phi Gamma," I tell her. She never remembers the Greek name.

"Those girls who asked you to join the sorority. Now they're smart girls, Sue. And they like you."

"I guess." I shrug my shoulders. I don't really believe they want me in their sorority.

"And you're in the French Club, too."

By now I am really crying.

"What is it, honey?" she asks, keeping her voice soft. "What's wrong?"

"How can they want me in a sorority when I live *here*?"

That's when I decide to tell her about Miss Rosa.

"The other day Miss Rosa told me I'd be lucky to finish high school."

Miss Maude looks startled. "Why would she say that?"

"She says I spend too much time going out with boys."

"She has no right to talk to you like that. No right at all. Besides, it's not true. Not at all."

"Well, that's what she said. And it's not the first time." I decide to tell her everything. "She says I'll end up pregnant and drop out. She says I'm 'no different.' I can see it in her eyes every time she looks at me."

"Sue, you have to ignore her."

"How can I? She's a housemother. She works in the cottage on your days off."

Miss Maude lights another cigarette. She looks at the floor.

I chew on my lip. I sure wish I could smoke in here.

"Sue, let's get this nonsense about Miss Rosa out of the way, all right?"

I don't answer.

"First off, she doesn't have any idea what kind of a person you really are." She shakes her head. "I don't know why she's doing it, Sue, but she's not speaking the truth. And you need to believe that."

I look at her, watch her face, watch her eyes. She's looking straight at me.

"Some people are bitter. And I think Miss Rosa is bitter. Can you understand that?"

I think about how Miss Rosa limps, how her hands shake all the time. How her eyes bulge behind her thick glasses. It's like she's always on the lookout for something.

"Yeah. I guess."

She brushes some ash off her lap. "Now let's get back to why you skipped school."

I sigh. I go back to the window and look out at the street. "I don't fit in at school. And I don't fit in here, either." I don't even mention how I don't fit in at Mom's place.

After a while I say, "I thought maybe it would be easier at the Home if I had Joy for a friend. She's so popular here."

I think about Joy and our time together yesterday.

When we skipped school, Joy and I sat on a big old log right on the edge of the river not far from North High. We got our feet wet, and the hem of my skirt was muddy. We were smoking my cigarettes. I was almost out. The sun was still warm, even though it was October. We were talking about boys, which Joy liked to do a lot.

"You like Nick, the football player, right?" Joy was giggling. "Or maybe you just hang around him so he'll carry all your books." She knew Nick walked me home from school some days. I didn't say anything.

Joy looked at me with her bright blue eyes. She was frowning. "You bring home too many books."

"He's nice," I told her. Then I added, "Maybe I should go to a football game."

Joy cracked up. "That would be a first. Miss Sue Pickering at a football game. You don't know the first thing about football."

She was right. I didn't, but Nick didn't seem to care about that.

Joy thought a bit. "Hey. You're taking French, right?" I nodded.

"What are you going to do with French? You going to take an airplane to Paris, Home girl?"

"Maybe."

"You'll be the one to get out of here, you know that?" She waved her cigarette around to show she meant not just the Home but the town. "But I won't. Nope."

She didn't sound too worried about it. Just annoyed. She moved her feet around in the water and took another puff. "I'll probably flunk out. And what do you wanna bet I get pregnant and end up marrying one of those greaseballs you make money off of playing pool down at Tony's?"

"It's for bus tokens," I reminded her.

She made a face. "Makes no difference." Then, after a while, "You going to join that stuck-up sorority?"

When I shrugged, she looked away from me, down the river.

It's dark out now. I'm back on the couch and Miss Maude is rocking gently in her chair near me. The sounds of after-dinner clean-up are over.

"Does Joy want to be your friend?" Miss Maude asks.

I think about that. I have to tell her the truth.

"I don't think she cares about me. Not at all."

Overwhelmed

As soon as the alarm goes off, I scramble around for the button. I don't even open my eyes. I know it's still dark out. It's only 5:30 and I hate it, but it's what I have to do.

I need to keep moving so I don't fall back to sleep. I yank on a pair of jeans and a worn out North High sweatshirt. I ignore my Geometry book that's still on the bedspread next to my little flashlight. I hate Geometry, but I do it. In the bathroom, I flick on the overhead so I can see to splash cold water on my face. My eyes look tired in the harsh light. Geez. Everything looks tired.

The house is quiet. I love that part of getting breakfast ready. I go downstairs to the kitchen and line up thirteen cereal bowls. It's winter, so I put a big pot of oatmeal on to cook before I take out the bread. Every morning, I make twenty-six pieces of toast, two for Miss Maude and two for each of the girls. I heat the water up for Miss Maude's coffee while I'm waiting for the oatmeal to bubble.

Sometimes I grab a cup to help me wake up before everyone comes pouring down the stairs.

I pick up a wooden spoon and stir the grainy oatmeal. As always, I think about school. Boy, Geometry just isn't making any sense to me. The teacher goes way too fast. And I'm getting my verbs mixed up during French and Latin.

Sometimes, while I'm sitting in French class or in Miss Canole's Social Studies class, I feel smart. Kids ask to see my homework. I'm not afraid to speak up. But sometimes it doesn't work out.

I think about last week when Miss Canole called on me. It was for public speaking. She gives us a topic every week. I keep stirring as the oatmeal begins to thicken.

"Let's begin with Sue," she announced.

Miss Canole calls on me a lot, and she always has nice things to say after I finish. She's real tall and wears a lot of super high heels. I like the purple ones the best. Her hair is short and bright red. The kids call her Bloody Mary Canole.

As soon as she said my name, I stood up and began the two-minute speech I had prepared. "Tomatoes are a fruit, but we like to eat them as vegetables. They are good raw as well as cooked. Lots of people around here grow tomatoes in their home gardens. It's a good . . . "

Out of the corner of my eye, I saw Miss Canole shaking her head. I stopped talking and looked around the room. Kids were covering their mouths so they wouldn't laugh out loud. A boy jabbed the guy sitting in front of him in the ribs with a pencil. Miss Canole rose and stood very tall behind her desk. Her voice sounded serious.

"Sue, what was the assigned topic for today's public speaking?"

By now, the room was quiet. A desk chair squeaked behind me.

"How to grow tomatoes?"

Miss Canole walked toward me. She had a piece of paper in her hand. She was frowning.

"Sue, what does this say?"

She pointed to a line at the top of the page. I read it out loud. "The Continent of Africa." The line about tomatoes was lower down on the page. It was for next week.

The room exploded in laughter. Miss Canole gave me a cold look. I could tell she was disappointed in her "good student."

"I'll have to give you a D, Sue. Next time," she said, "make sure you have the correct topic."

Kids were still giggling. When I sat down, Bonnie leaned over and tapped me on the shoulder.

"Hey Sue. Got a tomato?" she whispered.

I stir the oatmeal one more time. I lean over the kitchen counter to rest my head on my arms and close my eyes. After a minute or two, I get back to work. I tear open the bread wrapper and start making the twenty-six pieces of toast. With one hand, I stir the oatmeal to make sure it doesn't stick. I yawn.

As soon as the bread pops up, I put the next two slices in the toaster. After I butter the toast I put it on a cookie sheet. This way, I can keep it warm in the oven. Holding a box of kitchen matches in one hand, I open the oven door and lean in to turn on the gas.

Someone is yanking on my sweatshirt. My eyes are closed. I feel the cold concrete floor under my cheek.

"Get back, girls. Give her some room."

It's Miss Maude's voice. I turn my head and open my eyes just a little bit. She's standing over me. I am part way under the oven door.

Why am I on the floor?

"Did somebody check the gas?" It's Miss Maude again.

"Yes, Miss Maude," one of the girls answers.

"Sue? Are you all right?"

Somebody takes my hand. Joy helps me into a sitting position. Miss Maude cups my chin and looks hard into my eyes.

"Are you all right?" she asks again.

"I don't know." My voice sounds funny, like it's far away.

"Girls, are you sure the gas is off?"

"Yes Miss Maude." It's Evie.

"Can you tell me what happened, Sue?"

I start slow. "I was putting toast in the oven. You know. To keep it warm." I turn my head just a little and look into the open oven. I am sitting on the floor, and it's right at eye level. There's a big cookie sheet with two dried out pieces of toast sitting in there. I look up at Miss Maude and the tears start.

"Something happened," I tell her in a soft voice.

"Shhh. It's all right, dear." She sounds relieved. "You must have fainted."

"I'll finish making breakfast." It's one of the girls speaking, I don't know which one.

Miss Maude helps me stand up and leads me into the dining room where I sit down in one of the plastic chairs. I notice the table is set. Then I remember setting it the night before.

"You've been studying too hard." It's not a question. Miss Maude knows I work late at night with my small flashlight under the covers. "You're tired, Sue. I think you should stay home today."

I feel so worn out, I don't try to change her mind. After a while, I go upstairs and crawl under my blankets.

Why is everything so hard for me now? I'm a junior and I'm working hard and getting good grades, but for what? Where am I going? Maybe I'll never make it out of this dumb town. Or never get to go to college. Maybe I'll end up like Joy says she's going to, pregnant and married to some dropout, one of those "greaseballs" from Tony's.

I wipe the tears away with the edge of my pink blanket. Just get some sleep, girl, I tell myself. You need some sleep.

FINDING MY WAY

Tryouts

"**Y**ou seem to enjoy reading aloud in class. Maybe you'd like to try out for the spring play." Mrs. Blockburger, my English teacher, is looking at me. I can tell she's not sure if I'm going to like this idea. Bonnie, who sits next to me in English, is looking at me too.

I'm not sure either. All I know about the kids in the Drama Club is that they hang out in the storage room under the stairs and smoke. That part's cool.

Later on, Bonnie and I are walking through the crowded hall on our way to Typing class. She looks like those girls on TV who have nice families and parents who pay a lot of attention to them. I wish I had her soft, wavy hair. She's done a lot of stuff in school, like being in the Drama Club and singing in the Glee Club. I decide to ask her about tryouts.

"If I go to tryouts, what do I have to do?"

"Oh, you read different parts from the play. Mrs. Blockburger will tell you which ones. Most of the kids who get picked are already in the Drama Club, but sometimes Mrs. Blockburger picks new kids."

The idea of going on stage in front of an audience makes my stomach crawl. That's hard enough, but what if Mom comes to see me in a play and it turns out like my baptism? I stare at the floor while we keep walking. Geez, it would be great to be someone else for a while.

"Okay," I tell Bonnie as we walk into the Typing room. "I'll see you at tryouts." She grins.

After classes are over for the day, I go to the auditorium. It's almost empty. The air smells old, like nobody's opened the windows in here for a long time. Most of the lights are off. Mrs. Blockburger is down front talking to a group of kids. I start down the aisle, which looks about a mile long. Luckily there's an empty seat next to Bonnie. When I sit down, she gives me a nudge, like she's glad I'm there.

Mrs. Blockburger starts talking to all of us about the play.

"We're looking for students to play Mr. and Mrs. Anderson and their children. I'm sure you've all seen the show on television." Heads nod.

"What show?" I whisper to Bonnie.

"Father Knows Best," she whispers back.

"Oh wow, I know that show!" I tell her. "It's great."

I love how Mrs. Anderson wears a dress and high heels, even when she's vacuuming. And the kids are bratty but they still get almost everything they want, like new clothes and bikes. I don't know any families like the Andersons, but there must be some.

"There's a large cast, so everybody's got a good chance." Mrs. Blockburger looks around. "I see we have some new students who'll be trying out as well." She smiles in my direction. In my head, I hear

Mom's warning. "Blend in, Sue-Sue. Don't call attention to your-self, and there won't be any trouble." I squirm in my seat.

Mrs. Blockburger calls on two Drama Club members to start the tryouts. I watch them pick up scripts from a card table down front and go up the short staircase to the stage. Mrs. Blockburger tells them what parts they're reading and what page to turn to. Then she talks a little bit about that section of the play and about the characters.

"In this scene, Mr. Anderson is about to leave to play golf, and his son is asking him about building a raft." Or "In this scene, Betty, the older daughter, is distraught because her party dress has a tiny rip in the hem." Geez.

Some of the kids who read are pretty sure of themselves. I guess they've done this a lot. Others are shy. Mrs. Blockburger encourages the quiet ones.

"Speak up, Mary Lou. We want to hear you."

"Yes ma'am," Mary Lou answers and pushes her glasses up on her nose.

I'm still sitting in the back next to Bonnie when I hear my name.

"Sue? Would you read the part of Betty in this next scene, please?" She takes a script off the table and holds it out to me. Bonnie pretends to clap and gives me a huge smile. "You can do it, Sue," she whispers.

I swallow hard. Betty's the one with a rip in her hem. I take the script from Mrs. Blockburger and walk up on stage. Some girl I don't know reads the part of Mrs. Anderson. As we go back and forth with the lines, my voice sounds funny and sort of fake. When it's over, I drop the script on the little table and hurry back to my seat. I don't dare look at Bonnie.

A while later Mrs. Blockburger calls on me to read the same part again, this time with a different girl reading Mrs. Anderson. I try, but I don't sound much better. This Betty girl reminds me of a princess, and the words she says are silly. I take a quick glance at the teacher, but she's not showing anything. She's just watching.

I'm already down the steps ready to put the script back on the table when she stops me.

"Sue? Would you go back up on stage please? We're going to switch to a different scene. This time, would you read the part of Mrs. Anderson?"

I turn and walk back up the stairs. Mrs. Anderson? I race through my memory. Do I know anyone like this? All I can think of is that great movie star Donna Reed and how she always wears high heels and a shirtwaist dress, even in commercials.

"James?" Mrs. Blockburger looks around the group until she finds tall, handsome James with the dark hair. "I'd like you to go up and read Mr. Anderson again. And Bonnie, this time, would you read the daughter?" She gives us the page number, and the three of us begin turning pages to find it. James is a senior. Next to him, I feel short and dumpy and nervous. And here's beautiful Bonnie reading my daughter? You've got to be kidding.

As soon as we start to read, I don't know why, but this time, it's much better. The part of Mrs. Anderson feels natural, even though I've never worn a dress and high heels to clean the mud room. My voice is stronger. The words come out right. I look James in the eye. I don't feel dumpy any more. I don't know what's happening, but it's magic.

The next day, Bonnie tells me the cast list is posted on the bulletin board outside the auditorium.

My eyes get really big. "Did I . . . ?"

"Go see for yourself," she says, giggling.

I move quickly through the hall until I'm standing in front of the list. There's my name. And it's right next to "Mrs. Anderson." I whisper it out loud to myself just to be sure.

"Sue Pickering playing Mrs. Anderson."

And Bonnie's playing Betty!

Well, I'm not "blending in." But I am going to be Mrs. Anderson! The notice says rehearsals start next week. I reach into my purse to check my supply of bus tokens.

A real date night

It all gets started after math class one day. Hal and I are standing in the hallway groaning about Advanced Algebra when the bell rings. I start walking to my Latin class and Hal walks right beside me. He's done this a few times, so it isn't a total surprise. But then the next thing I know, he's asking if I'd like to go out. To *dinner*.

Hal's a little taller than I am and he's got a blond crew cut and bright blue eyes. I love the way he walks—it's like he knows where he's going.

I walk a little faster.

"Go out to dinner? But I live at the Home." I say this fast. I want him to know about this right up front. Hardly any boy wants to take a Home girl anyplace nice. When I look at him, he's nodding.

"Yeah, I know where you live," he says.

I stare at him for a minute. How does he know about the Home?

"Well, I need a pass to go out," I announce. "Would you believe, it takes three signatures just to leave the property!" I try to make it sound like I think it's funny. "I need one even to go to sorority meetings."

We're outside the Latin classroom now. We stand and look at each.

"Well, do you think you could get a pass? Maybe for Saturday? Then we could go have dinner."

Pause. I guess he means it.

"Sure. Maybe. I guess so. I'll try."

My signed pass is sitting on the hall table right next to the phone. Miss Maude is upstairs in my room helping me get ready. She pours through my closet and picks out a cranberry colored skirt and a rose-colored sweater set. She tells me this will be more than suitable for my first "dinner date."

"What if he takes me to a really fancy place?" I ask her while I pull on my skirt. "What if I don't know what all the things on the menu are?"

"Shhh," she says, turning me around to make sure my slip isn't showing. "You're worrying about nothing. We don't have many places like that here in Binghamton. And that's probably not where this nice young man is going to take you for dinner."

She doesn't really know he's a nice young man because she hasn't met him yet, but she's betting on it.

I'm standing there in my bare feet. "Stockings or socks?" I ask.

"Stockings. And those nice little black flats you hardly ever wear." That means no sneakers.

When we hear his car arrive, Miss Maude and I hurry over to the living room window. I want to watch Hal park his pale blue Karmann Ghia in front of the cottage. I can tell Miss Maude's impressed with the shiny sporty looking car. So am I.

When he comes down the walk, he moves like he does at school, like he's sure of himself. He's got on a light blue shirt and a dark blue blazer. And tan pants. With a crease. I bet he's from a ritzy family. He's probably the first *real* guy who's come to pick up a Home girl for a date.

"Oh Miss Maude, he's so cute. What am I going to talk about? What if—"

She turns me so I face her, putting her hands on my shoulders. "Sue, you're smart and you're pretty and you're going to have a wonderful time, so stop worrying."

He knocks, and she goes to open the front door.

I feel like a princess riding in Hal Blair's Karmann Ghia. I roll down the window. The wind starts blowing my hair around, but I don't care. The car is so cool, it would be like heaven to be riding in it, even if Hal wasn't just about the cutest boy at North High.

I hate to get out of the dream car, but we're here. The fancy sign outside this large wooden restaurant says it's called The Barn, which doesn't sound very fancy. When we get inside, it looks like I imagine a really nice barn would look, especially if it's in a movie. The walls are covered with wide planks of what could be old weathered wood. There's a high peaked roof and, at the other end of the room, I can see big sliding doors. When Hal parked, there were already lots of cars in the lot. People wearing fancy clothes and looking really rich were walking toward The Barn, smiling and talking. Boy, it feels like we're going to have dinner with a bunch of ritzy older people at a really fancy farm.

The light inside is dim. Hal steps forward to stand by what looks like a podium, so I go stand beside him. A woman in a black dress asks, "Do you have a reservation, sir?"

"Yes. Blair. For two."

The lady puts a checkmark next to Hal's name in a large note-book and leads us to a booth. There's a glowing candle in the center of the table and white cloth napkins.

I watch Hal as he talks to the waitress. He's been here before, I bet. And probably lots of other places like this. I wish I had worn a party dress, except I don't have one.

Our menus are huge and have different pages for different kinds of meals. I find the dinner page. Roast beef. Steak. Chicken in wine sauce. Lasagna.

"Everything is really good here," Hal tells me. "What kind of food do you like?"

My mind goes blank. I try to come up with something fancy to impress him. My head feels like an empty blackboard. For some reason, I think about Mom.

"I like steak," I tell him. "When I lived with my mom, she used to broil steak for us. She'd brush it with Italian dressing while it cooked. It was really good." I look down. "That was a long time ago."

Wow, that was stupid. What does Hal care about my mom broiling steak?

"That sounds great," he says scanning the menu. "Hey, here's a steak that's marinated before they cook it." He looks at me. "Want to try that? It may not be quite like your mom's, but I'll bet it's good."

"Yeah, that sounds great. We don't get a whole lot of steak at the Home."

We laugh.

Hal's telling me about his parents and where they're going for a vacation. It's an island called Antigua. I'm watching him talk and I'm trying to remember where the island is when the slippery water glass slides through my fingers and dumps ice water all over the table. Hal grabs his napkin and starts sopping it up. I build a dam with my napkin, trying to keep the water from pouring onto my lap. The waitress hurries over right away, blotting and sopping with us.

I hardly have time to feel foolish, it happens so fast. After the waitress brings us new place settings and new water glasses, Hal and I start to laugh. I'm red in the face, I know, but we're still laughing.

"Good thing it happened before your steak came, huh?" he says.

"Yeah, good thing."

I lean against the back of the tall wooden booth and listen to Hal's story about going on a camping trip. And then he asks about my part in the school play, and we talk about "Father Knows Best." I can tell he's kind of impressed that I'm in the play. "I'd never make it up there on the stage," he tells me. "I'm not what you'd call 'creative.'"

After a while, when our salad arrives, Hal asks me, "So what's it like, living at the Home?"

I remember talking with Charles in Florida. I think how good and solid Hal seems to be. And so I tell him some of the good things about the Home. And some of the bad things.

The shafted club

The Wigwam windows are so steamy, I can hardly see who is inside. A bunch of kids are hanging out by the counter waiting for seats. The booths are packed. Standing outside on the sidewalk, I can hear Ricky Nelson singing "Poor Little Fool." I look down at my faded skirt and my saddle shoes. They're okay, I guess. I'm just glad it's warm enough out so I didn't have to wear that black leather jacket.

The Wigwam is where the popular kids go after school. At least, I think they're popular. Sometimes somebody invites me to come along, but that's only once in a blue moon. But today it's Friday, and I have a message to deliver to Bonnie about Monday's rehearsal.

Through the window, I see Hal over by the soda fountain. And Rich from the Drama Club is laughing with a bunch of his friends. Bonnie's there too, sitting in the back. I bet she's drinking her usual cherry cola. I sure wish I had her long wavy hair. The perm that Miss Maude gave me is so curly, I look like one of those cartoon characters who stuck his finger in the electric outlet.

As soon as I open the door, a guy standing next to the jukebox drops a nickel in and "Wake Up Little Susie" comes on. They play this sometimes when I come in. They have songs they play for some of the other girls, too. It embarrasses me, but secretly I think it's sort of nice. At least they know who I am.

Hal waves. I wave back. He was nice when I told him I wasn't ready to be boyfriend-girlfriend.

"Don't worry, Sue. It's okay. We can be friends for now. And maybe someday . . . ." He shrugged and grinned without finishing his sentence.

I didn't want to try and explain. I was afraid that, if he really knew me, he wouldn't want to be around me at all. I could talk about the Home, but how could I ever tell him, or anyone, about the time I got in a fight with my Mom and hit her? Or how the girls beat me up until I smashed Sharon's head against the hair dryer? What if he found out that Mom showed up drunk at my baptism?

Hal calls out to me. "Hey, how's Algebra going?"

I walk toward him so I don't have to yell over the crowd.

"Not good," I answer. "But it should turn out okay."

"Yeah, for you," Hal says. "McGinnis really likes you."

I don't know what to say. I think maybe it's true, but I know it's not right. I want good grades because I'm a good student, not because the teacher really likes me.

"Well, I hope I do okay on the Regents exam."

"Yeah." Hal looks at me. "You worry too much, Sue. You'll do all right."

"Hey, Susie." It's one of the guys leaning on the jukebox. Everyone knows I hate to be called Susie. I ignore him and hurry toward the back of the Wigwam to find Bonnie.

I'm dodging around kids, left and right, when I hear a familiar voice. "Hey, Sue, how are rehearsals going?"

I look up. It's Rich, from the Drama Club. He's tall and has a big smile.

"Okay, I guess." I feel too shy to tell him I really like being in the play.

"I hear you're playing Mrs. Anderson."

"Yeah." I look down. I can feel my cheeks start to burn. I want to talk about the play, but by the time I look up, he's gone.

I find Bonnie and tell her about the change in rehearsal time for Monday. Then we giggle about how ancient our costumes make us look, and I tell her the high heels I'm wearing in the show make my feet hurt, and stuff like that. Girl talk. Boy, I never thought I'd get to do that!

When it gets close to time for my bus, I start toward the door. As I squeeze through the crowd, one of the jukebox boys raises his voice.

"Look at her, would you? Miss Snooty. She's the one with The Shafted Club. She's turned down every guy at North High." Somebody laughs.

I keep moving. There is no Shafted Club. None of this is true, but these jerky boys like to try to get my attention.

"Susie's Shafted Club." Now he's talking really loud. "You heard about it, right? It's for all the guys who tried but didn't make it. Like Hal over there. And that guy who asked her to the prom last winter, and she said no. What's his name?"

I keep walking. They're like hornets, I tell myself. Don't listen to them. And I feel so bad about not becoming Hal's girlfriend.

But I don't know how to *have* a boyfriend! I can't imagine what it's like. Part of me is scared about what guys will do to a Home girl. Or what they expect from me. I can still hear Miss Rosa's voice. "You're no different. You'll get pregnant and have to drop out, just like the rest of them."

I open the Wigwam door and take a deep breath of cool air.

Photo Queen

Miss Maude came to see the play in May just before it closed. She said I was a "lovely" Mrs. Anderson. Mrs. Blockburger liked me, too. "Good job, Sue," she told me. I probably shouldn't have been so relieved, but Mom didn't come.

It's September and school has started. I always love that part. I'm in the living room with an older couple named Don and Elaine Burgess. They're photographers. Several other girls and I are sprawled on the floor, and Miss Maude is settled in her favorite brown chair. On the carpet, the couch, and the end table, there are piles of photos of me. It feels really weird to see my face everywhere. Here's me smiling, now I'm waving, here I'm climbing up on rocks, looking at clouds, you name it. Don took the pictures, and Elaine brought all the lights and props and whatever else was needed. She's real quiet and friendly and helps me feel comfortable about all this.

Last spring, when they came by to take photos of Home kids, they ended up asking me to be their "model" so they could enter some contest. I was nervous about trying this, but Miss Maude said it was okay, so I got to spend time with the Burgesses on weekends. We even spent a whole week together during the summer. We drove up to Maine to be by the ocean while they took pictures. It was so cool to be near the ocean again. I told them about going to Florida that time, but I didn't talk about Ronnie.

I paw through some of the photos on the floor. There I am, standing on a huge rock staring into the distance. And here's one where I'm in front of a bridge wearing a silly Caribbean skirt, smiling and waving. They've got pictures of me looking up, looking down, sitting, standing, staring into the camera. They sure don't look special to me, but Don and Elaine seem to be very happy. They're picking the ones to enter as slides in the contest.

"I'm betting on this one," Elaine says holding up a print. "What do you think, Sue?"

Oh boy. There are my dark heavy eyebrows over my light brown eyes. My cheeks are so round they look puffy. I can't help but notice that my smile is higher on one side than the other. My hair looks like I took tight little curlers out and never combed it. I look over at Elaine and shrug my shoulders.

It's October when Elaine calls me.

"Sue, we won! We won the contest." Her voice pops out of the phone.

"We did?" I want to run upstairs to tell Miss Maude, but I need to find out more. "What happens now?"

"Well, your face is going to be in the newspaper. You're the Photo Queen!" My thoughts are running around like the balls on the pool table down at Tony's. "And there's a big fancy banquet to honor you and the Photo Princess," Elaine tells me. "And, since you're the queen, you get to sit on a throne."

Wow! A throne! Visions of the Miss America contest pop into my head. "What do I have to wear, Elaine?" I hope a whole lot that it's not a bathing suit.

"A fancy dress. We'll find something. Don't worry." Her voice gets serious. "Congratulations, Sue. And thanks for being such a great sport all these months."

When Elaine stops by after dinner a few days later, I want to show her the dress Miss Maude and I picked out. Somehow, last year the Home got a store to donate some prom dresses. Miss Maude and I chose one of these for the Photo Queen banquet. Maybe I'll get to wear it to a real prom someday. It's white with a wide red sash, and it has lots and lots of netting. I picked out some prom shoes, too, which came to the Home along with the dresses. Elaine waits while I dig out the white high heels that have plastic over the toes and put them on.

Elaine looks at me in the fancy dress and the cool shoes and claps her hands in approval. "This will be sort of like a prom, Sue, only you'll be sitting on a throne."

After she leaves, Miss Maude gives me a hug. "I'm so proud of you, honey," she says. "Now go get your beauty rest."

The girls are quiet upstairs for once. I close my door and sit down on the edge of my bed. It's the first time I've won anything. Well, except for being salutatorian when I graduated from Junior High. I hang up what I now think of as my Photo Queen dress and make sure the netting isn't wadded up. Then I put the white shoes side by side right in the front of the closet.

Later that week, I meet Mom after school. Somehow, we always end up sitting at the soda counter at Woolworths. After I take a big sip of my lemon cola, I tell her about being chosen as the Photo Queen. I try not to make a big deal about it.

"Sue, that's wonderful! You deserve it, sweetheart." I think I see tears in her eyes. "Is there going to be a party?"

I wait. I want to tell her I don't know, but it's not true. But I'm scared she'll want to come. I think about the time she showed up drunk at my baptism.

"It won't be that special, Mom. Other people are getting awards, too. And besides, I'll have to sit with Mr. and Mrs. Burgess all the time. They're the photographers."

She takes a scrap of paper out of her purse. "I want to write down the date so I'll be sure to remember."

I light a cigarette, take a drag, and tell her the date.

The hall is packed with tables covered with white tablecloths. There are bowls of flowers and balloons everywhere. My shoes pinch like mad, and I don't care.

A man in a white jacket with a flower in his lapel walks us to our table at the front of the room. It's up on a platform that's next to a little stage. The Photo Princess is sitting there. She turns to smile at me. She's really pretty. Boy, I wonder how she ended up the princess and me the queen. I push that out of my head.

Everybody gets a chicken dinner with canned peas, which is only a little better than we have at the Home. We eat and listen to speeches about things like F stops and lighting. Finally, the same man in the white jacket goes up on the little stage that's right next to our table and taps on the microphone.

"And now, folks, the moment you've all been waiting for." He looks over at us with a huge smile. His face is shiny. "First, let's have a big round of applause for our winners, Don and Elaine Burgess, for entering their slides in our contest." The audience claps. Somebody whistles.

"And now," he says, looking at me, "would our Photo Queen please take the throne?"

Music starts to play. It's "A Pretty Girl Is Like a Melody." It makes me really nervous, so I turn to Elaine. She takes my hand and walks me over to the stage and up a few steps to the throne. Well, it isn't really a throne. It's a big chair with a high back that's covered with yellow and blue and pink fake flowers. It looks really nice. After I'm seated, the white-jacket guy comes over and places a tiny rhinestone crown on my head. When he stands back, they turn up the music. The audience starts clapping like mad. I can't help but smile.

Pretty soon, the lights dim and softer music comes on. That's when Don and Elaine's first slide of me appears. There I am, a giant face on a screen. The picture stays for what feels like forever, then fades away and another comes on. In this one, I'm standing by a garden and holding a flower. My hand looks so big, I start to giggle. In the next one, there's my huge face looking right at the camera. It's so big, I can see the pores on my nose! I glance over at Don. He's looking at me, smiling and pretending he's taking my picture on the throne.

Finally the slide show ends and the lights come on. The announcer starts talking, but I'm not listening. I'm watching a woman walk slowly down the aisle. She moves like she's trying to keep her balance. She's crying. "My baby," she calls out, looking up at me. "My beautiful baby!"

I am glued to the throne. As she walks unevenly past people sitting near the aisle, they stare at her. Don stands up. "Is that your mom?" Elaine mouths to me. I nod.

Don steps off the platform where we're sitting and walks up the aisle toward her. He moves with ease, like everything is normal, like it's all okay. I watch him lean over and say something to her. She stares up at him. All the time, he's smiling. He gently puts his hand on her elbow and helps her turn around. Together, they begin to walk toward the exit. Don is nodding and talking to my mother. When she stumbles, my heart freezes. But Don tightens his grip on her arm and steadies her. Somehow, even to me, he looks like he's escorting an important person.

People everywhere in the auditorium are standing and putting on their coats. They're all smiles as they talk and laugh with each other. No one is paying attention to my mom. Elaine comes over to me still sitting on the throne and softly places her hand on my shoulder.

"Are you okay?" Her voice is low, concerned.

"I guess so." I look up at her. "How will she get home?"

"Don't worry, Sue. Don will get her a cab."

After a minute, she smiles. "Ready to go?"

I stand up from my throne, still in my rhinestone crown. Elaine reaches for my hand.

THE DOOR OPENS

The first step

"**I**'m going to work in summer stock again this year," Rich announces. He looks smug.

He's sitting across from me in a booth in the Wigwam, with his long legs stuck out in the aisle. It's the middle of May. I'm half-way through my senior year and school is almost out for summer. Kids are talking about their summer plans. I don't have any.

"What's summer stock?"

It's so loud in here, it's hard to hear. The air is blue. Almost everybody smokes. My Pall Malls are on the table next to my lemon cola. Rich pulls one out of my pack. Dues for telling me about summer stock.

"Have you ever been to the Masonic Temple downtown to see any of the plays?"

I shake my head. I don't bother explaining that Home kids don't go to the theater much.

"Well, in the summer, there's a different show every week. Professional actors come to town and bring costumes and special props, and us local apprentices help build the sets and put on the show. Sometimes they even bring their own assistants or their dressers. And these are famous actors, you know? They've been on Broadway and in the movies." He's really excited now. "This summer, Tallulah Bankhead's going to be here. And Victor Jory. He played that really bad guy, the overseer, in *Gone with the Wind*. And Hermione Gingold." He's waiting for a reaction. "Hey, even Sir Cedric Hardwicke is coming. You remember him, right? He's in that movie, *Around the World in Eighty Days*. And he's in *The Ten Commandments*."

I'm impressed. Real actors in this boring old factory town of Binghamton? I don't know who they are, but I want to hear more. I lean forward. "What's it like to work there?"

"Well, last summer was my first time. I'm an apprentice. We do all the grunt work—you know, build sets, run errands, clean the green room—stuff like that." He seems a little embarrassed. "It's not glamorous, that's for sure." His eyes brighten. "But we get to see really good actors at work. And sometimes we get to play bit parts in their shows."

I sit up straight. "Oh wow. Do you think I could do it? I'd love to have a part in a play, but I don't know much about building sets or the other stuff."

"Oh, you'd do fine, Sue. Carl's a great teacher. He's the House Carpenter. I bet you'd learn fast. Heck, it's no pay and you work like a dog, but you learn a lot about the theater."

He takes a drag on his Pall Mall. "Do you want me to get you an interview?"

DO I WANT AN INTERVIEW?

My heart races around in my chest, but I try to look cool. "Hey, Rich. Thanks. I would love to have an interview. If you'd help me get ready. I mean, I don't know what they want to know. Or anything." I try to stop squirming around in the booth.

"Okay. Sure." He pauses. He looks a little awkward. "Will the Home let you do this?"

"Oh, it'll be all right," I tell him. But I know this is going to be like asking to go to the moon.

I pick up my Pall Malls, wave good-bye, and run for the bus.

That night, I talk to Mac and Miss Maude about being an apprentice. I tell them everything Rich told me. Experienced actors. Building sets. Hard work. I mention some names.

"Rich says this summer, the theater's going to have Arthur Treacher and Victor Jory and Hermione Gingold."

Their eyebrows go up. They're nodding at each other now. Good. They know who these actors are.

"And Tallulah Bankhead is coming." Miss Maude rolls her eyes. I move right on.

"And an actor named Sir Cedric Hardwicke."

Their faces relax.

Okay, we're back on track.

"What about getting paid?" Mac asks. "Do they pay apprentices?"

"No. I won't get paid." I am worried about this part. "But I'll get *lots* of experience."

I'm not exactly sure what that means, but I want to find out.

Mac and Miss Maude look at each other. They don't say much, but I can tell they're concerned. I try to keep my leg from jiggling.

Finally, Mac speaks. "Well, this may help you figure out whether you really want to be an actress. It's not an easy life, you know."

Miss Maude is frowning a bit, but her eyes sparkle.

"You make sure you don't let those theater people take advantage of you," she says waving her finger in the air. "You're young, Sue, and . . . well, you need to take care."

The Dutchman

My mind is blurry. I'm hardly getting any sleep. Most days, I'm running from late morning until after the show ends. Sometimes I see Rich, but lots of times I'm working with people I hardly know or on my own. Everything is new. It's scary—and I'm loving it.

I learned right away that as soon as I finish one job, I'm to show up at Carl's elbow for orders. He's called our House Carpenter, but he keeps track of everything.

"Sue, run this hat box over to costumes. They need it pronto."

"Sue, can you get me some coffee, black?"

"Hey, Sue, this button came off his costume. Can you fix it?"

"Sue, they need you on script. When one of the actors yells 'Line,' feed it to them."

I like working for him. He's quiet and even-tempered, and, in spite of the chaos, each show ends up looking spiffy, as Mom would say. He isn't theatrical about it, either. He's easy to be around.

I've only been here a few days, and tryouts are coming up already. There's a part for a young girl in *The Happiest Millionaire*. I'd be on stage with Victor Jory, who Miss Maude says "makes her swoon." Carl and Peter, the Stage Manager, both say I should read for it. I don't tell them that auditioning makes me feel like throwing up. Every time I audition, I hear Mom's warning in my head. "If you don't want to get hurt, Sue-Sue, stay out of the limelight. The less people notice you, the better off you'll be."

I remember her advice. But I do it anyway. I figure this time, I'll go throw up in the ladies room early and get it over with. It'll be worth it if I get the part.

We're getting ready for *Visit to a Small Planet* when Carl calls me over.

"We're behind on building the set, Sue. Can you go down below and patch holes in the old flats for me? Use a Dutchman."

I nod and run for the stairs. I have no idea what a Dutchman is.

"Down below" is a big room under the auditorium where we build a different set every week. It's always hot down here and smells like paint thinner. I open the door and climb over paint cans, glue pots and brushes. Scenery is stacked helter-skelter against the walls. Parts of sets lie in bits and pieces on the floor.

I'm wandering around the room trying to imagine what I am supposed to be doing with a Dutchman when I hear the door open. There's a man standing there. He is tall and angular, and his profile looks like it belongs on a Roman coin.

He looks around the room. "Must be the set for next week's show," he mutters. Then he asks, "Do you work here?" His voice is different. Maybe he's British.

"I'm an apprentice." I look around at the mess. "I'm supposed to be mending holes in these flats. Carl said to use a Dutchman." I'm too tired to fake it. "But I don't know what a Dutchman is." I almost don't care if he notices tears of frustration starting.

"Well," he says, "I may be a bit long in the tooth for this sort of thing, but I'd be happy to lend you a hand." He looks at me. Long in the tooth must mean getting old, but he sounds like he knows about this Dutchman thing. I nod.

"Well, let's see what we've got here." He whistles softly as he walks around the room, stepping over pails and examining pieces of scenery.

"Ah, here we are." He picks up a large piece of muslin and begins tearing it into strips. My hand flies to my mouth in surprise.

"Are we supposed to do that?" I ask. What if he's some crazy man who wandered in from the street, and here I am letting him rip up our muslin?

In a moment, he holds up a rectangular piece of cloth about one foot wide and two feet long. "This, my young apprentice, is called a Dutchman," he tells me. "And it is what we're going to use to patch the holes in the set."

"Oh wow. You know how to do this!" He's smiling. I start to laugh. "Are you Carl's assistant or something?" I ask.

"No, love, just passing through." Definitely British.

He drags over a glue pot and a brush and kneels down. Then he paints glue along the edges of a rip in the flat. "But I can tell you this, my young friend. I certainly do need a set for next week."

"You need a set?"

"Forgive me, my dear. I haven't properly introduced myself." It takes a minute for him to unwind so that his tall body is standing before me. "My name is Arthur Treacher. I'm 'starring,' as you Americans like to say, in *Visit to a Small Planet*, which opens next week."

The door swings wide and Carl rushes in, clipboard in hand. His eyes grow large as they shift back and forth between his brand new apprentice and the star of next week's show, who is holding a glue pot.

"Uh, Mr. Treacher, sir," he says, while gently taking the glue pot. "Whatever brought you down below?" Now Carl is glaring at me as though I'd kidnapped this man, dragged him downstairs, and beat him until he helped me patch holes in the scenery.

"Oh, just wandering around, old boy. Say, you must be Carl."

Mr. Treacher looks down at me with a happy smile. "I came across our friend here, and it seemed as though she could use a bit of help."

He looks back at Carl. "My apologies if I've upset the routine. Making the Dutchman was my idea, you see. I used to do quite a bit of this sort of thing in my younger days. Always enjoyed it."

Mr. Treacher turns to me and makes a small bow. "Well, my dear, I guess I'm being banished to rehearsal. Good luck with your Dutchman."

Carl and I listen to his whistle as Mr. Treacher starts up the stairs.

"For God's sake, Sue, that's Arthur Treacher. He's starring in the next show." Carl sounds tired. "Opens in four days. That is, if we have a set." Yup. Definitely tired.

I can't wait to tell Miss Maude about this. She's going to love this story.

"Virginia is heah"

Once we have Arthur Treacher on stage, our attention goes to next week's show. I don't know how it happens, but this one brings Tallulah Bankhead all the way to our boring little town. Everybody's talking about her.

"I hear she makes up lines. Leaves the actors hanging. Drives 'em crazy."

"Yeah. And she drinks a lot. And *not* just off-stage."

"I bet she's gonna want a lot of favors—special lighting, new props, you name it."

I'm backstage with the rest of the crew getting ready for Miss Bankhead and listening to these stories. Peter, the Stage Manager, saunters over to me.

"Hey, Sue. I need someone to work with Tallulah Bankhead next week. I think you'd be perfect for the job." He's grinning.

"Oh boy, *that* sounds like fun." I have learned there's no such thing as being perfect for any job. I'm just standing in the wrong place at the wrong time.

Peter points to the steep, narrow staircase Carl is painting. "You see these stairs?" I nod. "Miss Bankhead's got to climb these pretty much in the dark. Then she has to wait on the platform at the top until she hears her cue. We want you with her to make sure she doesn't have any mishaps."

Mishaps? I stare at Carl.

"Don't worry, Sue," he says. "If anything happens, give us a sign, and we'll bail you out."

Peter nods. "It'll be okay, kiddo. I'm always in the wings if you need me."

I think about it. "Okay," I tell him. I want to help him out, and besides, Peter's really cute with shiny black hair and dark eyes.

It's Saturday afternoon and I'm wandering around backstage, looking for a quiet place to sit down before dress rehearsal. I turn a corner and find a short, round black woman bending over an ironing board humming to herself. She has on a trim black dress and a starched white apron and cap. I stop about five feet away.

"Where did *you* come from?" she asks, startled to see me there. Her dark wide forehead is shiny with sweat and her glasses are part way down her nose.

"I work here," I explain. "My name's Sue. I'm an apprentice." I'm staring at the reddish-gold dress on her ironing board. The material shimmers.

"Pretty, huh." She smoothes the fabric with her hand. "Miss Bankhead wears this in the party scene, when she comes down the stairs and all the men are watching." The woman closes her eyes for a moment. I imagine she's thinking about Miss Bankhead making that entrance. Oh boy, so am I.

When she slips the dress off the board, it sparkles like it's covered with tiny rhinestones.

"It's so beautiful."

"Miss Bankhead has a lot of pretty costumes. You'll see." Then she announces, "I'm Rose. Miss Bankhead's personal dresser." Rose slides the glittery gown onto a hanger.

Wow! I've never met a personal dresser before.

"So, Sue, what's your job during Miss Bankhead's show?"

I take a deep breath before I answer.

"The Stage Manager asked me to help Miss Bankhead backstage. You know, when she climbs the stairs for her big entrance. Is there anything special I should know?"

Rose looks like she doesn't understand my question. I try again.

"I mean, it's just that the staircase is dark and narrow, and she'll be in a gown and high heels. So . . . is Miss Bankhead nervous about heights or anything?"

Rose throws her head back and laughs. Her teeth are bright white.

"Lord no, girl. That woman ain't afraid of nothin'. You'll see."

The next day before dress rehearsal, I overhear Miss Bankhead complaining to Carl about "that damn staircase." When he shrugs his shoulders and turns away, she starts in on Peter. He nods reassuringly, but I can't hear what he's saying. I stay out of sight.

By early evening, TB, as I now think of her, is pretty heated up. Carl and I watch as she yells and tosses one of Rose's neatly ironed costumes on the floor.

"It's going to be a long week, Sue," Carl whispers. "You be careful on those stairs." He pats me on the shoulder and leaves.

Watching TB stamp her feet and wave a cigarette around, I try to imagine getting her up those stairs and not getting killed in the process. The prospect doesn't look good.

When dress rehearsal starts, I sit down backstage next to Rose. She's got her sewing basket at her feet, and there's a skirt across her lap. She pulls out a spool of red thread and a needle.

"Hi, Rose," I say. My backstage whisper sounds nervous.

"Hello there," she answers softly.

We listen for a while to the deep male voices coming from the stage.

"Where's Miss Bankhead?" I whisper. "Isn't it almost time for her to go on?"

"Oh, she'll be here." Rose threads the needle.

I look at the reddish-gold dress hanging on the rack.

"She doesn't wear costumes for rehearsals," Rose tells me, knowing I'm expecting to see that dress go on stage.

Right about then we hear a crash like someone walked into one of the flats in the wings. I start to jump up. Rose grabs my arm and shakes her head. We wait.

Soon we hear a loud Southern stage whisper. "Rose, goddamn it, where *are* you?"

Rose sighs, puts down her mending and walks into the dark toward the voice. She returns leading a pale thin woman with giant eyes and auburn hair that reaches her shoulders.

"Shhh, Miss Bankhead, everything's fine, you come with me," she murmurs as she guides the actress in my direction.

TB has a lit cigarette in one hand and an empty glass in the other. A dark wet spot is spreading down the outside of one leg of her perfectly tailored white slacks.

"Miss Bankhead," Rose whispers, "This here's Sue. She's going to help you on the stairs."

Miss Bankhead ignores me and takes a deep drag on her cigarette as Rose begins blotting the liquor stain.

I am embarrassed. Off balance. Like when Mom shows up drunk. I am clenching my teeth.

"Damn it, Rose, forget that." TB pushes Rose's hand away. "Just get me a drink."

Rose pulls a silver flask from the bottom of her sewing basket, unscrews the top, and pours a large drink into Miss Bankhead's glass.

I watch TB take a deep swallow.

She's rude and drunk and smoking, and I have to get her up those stairs. I look around. No sign of Peter or Carl.

TB closes her eyes as she listens to the dialog on stage. Suddenly her eyes pop wide open. "Shit, I'm on," she hisses. She grinds her cigarette out with her shoe and starts unevenly toward the staircase. The now half-empty glass is still in her right hand.

"For God's sake, whatever your name is," she declares, snapping her fingers in my direction. "Get over here."

I walk toward her, my heart thumping. As we start up the dark stairs, Miss Bankhead grabs my arm with her left hand. Her nails bite into my skin. She continues to hold her glass tight in the other. She ignores the railing.

She is small beside me. Wiry, like Mom.

She climbs rapidly, awkwardly. I remember helping Mom cross the street, feeling her hand on my arm, knowing she could fall. I straighten my shoulders and put my foot on the next step.

By the time we reach the platform at the top of the stairs, we're in darkness. I can hear TB breathing as she leans against the door to the stage, listening. Suddenly, she gulps the rest of her drink and shoves the glass into my hand. I jump back away from the door, my free hand scrambling for the railing. She flings the door open, pausing in dramatic splendor at the top of the on-stage staircase.

"Dahlings." Her Southern voice is deep and commanding. "Virginia is heah."

Where I belong

Peter and I sit on the edge of the stage, legs dangling. It's late, and the light is dim. The rest of the crew is gone. We're almost ready for next week's show, *The Happiest Millionaire*, with Victor Jory.

"They're not *all* like Tallulah," he tells me. His voice is quiet. "She's pretty hard core."

"You know," I say, thinking about the past week, "Rose made it okay. We talked a lot while she ironed and mended. And that whole week, she never said anything bad about Miss Bankhead. I respect her for that."

Just like I don't want to say anything bad about Mom. It's hard sometimes.

I see Peter's cigarette glow in the dark as he takes a drag. There's a coffee can between us, half-filled with butts.

"Hey, congratulations on your audition," he announces. "You did a terrific job." I feel his eyes on me. "It's great that you got the part."

"Thanks." I'm glad he can't see me blushing. I'm so nervous about getting out on this gigantic stage with a bunch of professional actors, I could faint. And Victor Jory is Miss Maude's favorite! Geez.

"That costume you wear is pretty cute, too. I like the long skirt and the big hat." Peter chuckles.

I like Peter. Even when something goes wrong backstage and the rest of the crew is going nuts, he smiles and keeps on track. He's a perfect Stage Manager. His hair is blue-black and shiny. To me, he looks like he's in his twenties, but I don't know for sure. Anyway, I think maybe he likes me. And he's soooo handsome.

I reach for a cigarette to make me stop thinking about Peter.

"What's Victor Jory like?" I ask.

"He's a nice guy. At least, that's what I hear. Hey, don't worry." He leans over and pokes me in the ribs. "You're only allowed one Tallulah Bankhead per season."

Yeah. Right.

The actors arrived in town yesterday on a huge bus, and our show opens tomorrow. I'm waiting on stage for Mr. Jory so we can go through my scenes. I sure hope it goes okay. He told Peter he wanted to see me in costume, so I put on the long pale green dress and the wide-brimmed hat that Peter likes. The empty auditorium is so enormous, I can't see all the way to the back. I imagine it filled with people, and my stomach does a serious flip-flop.

Take a deep breath, I tell myself. You don't want to throw up here.

I walk around Carl's set, mumbling my lines to myself. I touch the antique writing desk and sit down for a second on the chaise. There's a beautiful red and gold rug. Peter says it's Oriental. It feels soft, even with my shoes on.

After a while, I see Mr. Jory hurrying down the aisle toward the stage. He's wearing a sport coat and a narrow tie. He looks quite "dashing," as Miss Maude would say. He's tall and dark and dramatic looking. You can't help but notice him.

As soon as he reaches the stage, I hear Peter's voice over the PA system. "Good evening, Mr. Jory. Sue, let's take it from your first entrance, upstage left. Mr. Jory, you're at the writing desk. Places, please." My heart is now in my mouth.

We go through my scenes, and somehow I remember all my lines and manage to not trip on my long dress. "Good job, Sue," Mr. Jory says as he's leaving. I smile and give him a wave before I start back to the dressing room. I'm feeling pretty good when I hear a man's voice call out to me.

"Hey. You playing the cousin?" I see a man standing behind the same ironing board Rose used last week. He's pushing the iron around on what looks like a man's shirt.

"Yes, I am. Hi, I'm Sue."

"Jake."

"Are you Mr. Jory's dresser?"

He stares at me for a minute. Then he looks down at the iron in his hand and laughs.

"No, kid. No way." He shakes his head. "You wouldn't know it, but I'm a fighter."

I don't know what to say about that, so I start to move on. His voice reaches me as I'm almost in the dressing room.

"That is, I used to be a fighter. A hell of a fighter. But now." He pauses for a second like he's thinking something over. "I guess I'm an actor." He laughs out loud.

I turn around. "Are you in the play?"

"Yeah. I play the driver. But they call me the chauffeur."

His smile is uneven and his eyes twinkle. His skin looks rough. He makes me think of a young, hard-working Santa Claus, without the white hair and beard.

"You used to be a fighter?" I ask, returning to look at him across the ironing board.

"Yeah." He stands the iron on end and steps back. Suddenly he crouches down and begins punching the air, dodging and weaving, all from behind the ironing board. Then he stands up straight, his arms at his sides.

"Jake LaMotta, Miss. At your service."

For some reason, this strikes us both as funny. We laugh, and Jake slaps his leg. I keep my hand over my mouth so my fillings won't show.

Later, after I change out of my costume, I find Peter waiting for me by the light board.

"I met a nice guy named Jake," I tell him. "He's in the show. His last name's LaMotta. He says he was a fighter."

Peter grins. "Know what they call him?"

We're walking toward the exit now. I shake my head.

"The Raging Bull. Can you believe that? Jake LaMotta, The Raging Bull." He says it loud like he's an announcer.

"He seems really nice."

Peter laughs. "He probably is. Out of the ring."

During the week while I'm waiting to go on, sometimes I sit with Jake on the bench we keep backstage. He likes to talk, so mostly I listen. One night, he asks how old I am.

"Sixteen," I tell him. "But not for long. My birthday's this week."

"What day?" he asks.

"The sixteenth."

"Hey! Mine's the tenth," he replies. We grin. After Jake makes his entrance, I lean back against the wall, close my eyes, and wait for my cue. I think about birthdays.

The summer I turned nine, Mom and I lived at a school where she had somehow gotten a job as a housemother. This was a nice boarding school, not a place like the Home. On my birthday, I took a walk down the hill behind the house where we lived to lie in the grass under my favorite tree. I wanted to be alone, to think about what it would mean to be nine. Would it be different than eight? I hoped I'd be smarter, more grown up, but I didn't think so.

"Sue? Where aaa-re you? We're looking for you."

The girl's words were sing-song, like when you're playing hide-and-seek. I flipped over on my stomach, raised myself up on my hands and looked up the hill.

Sonia, a sophisticated teenager, was standing by the back door of our house. She had her hands on her hips. Her dark hair was whirling around in the wind. She was really tan, just like my mom. One night, another girl who lived in our house told me Sonia was Toscanini's granddaughter. Back then, I didn't know who that was. Now I do.

"I'm over here," I yelled to her. I stood up and waved my arms so she could see me in the high grass.

Sonia laughed as she started down the hill toward me. "I see you, you little imp," she called to me.

I always liked listening to her talk. She had a funny accent, kind of dramatic sounding. She told me her father came from Russia and he played the piano. "His name is Vladimir Horowitz. Have you heard of him?"

I shook my head.

"He's very famous. But no matter." Sonia looked bored, talking about her father.

She held out her hand to me. "Come here, come here, birthday girl. No more hiding today." We began our climb up the hill. She was smiling. Sometimes, when she talked, it was like she was singing.

I skipped along beside her into the kitchen. When she began to open the door that led to the living room, I stopped. Maybe something good was waiting in there for my birthday. Maybe not. Sonia gently put her hand on my shoulder and moved me toward the open door.

I remember that day, that time, even today, when I'm turning seventeen.

"Happy birthday, Sue," Peter whispers in my ear just before I set foot on stage. I'm so surprised, my first line flies out of my head for a second!

Somehow I manage to float through the evening. Being on stage for my seventeenth birthday feels like a huge present all by itself.

Then comes the curtain call. We're standing in a line taking our bows, when Mr. Jory steps out in front of us. He raises his arms and signals the audience to be quiet. The applause stops. Two women in the cast turn toward me and smile.

Mr. Jory's voice fills the theater, all the way to the back row. "We're celebrating a special occasion tonight." He turns and holds out his hand to me to step forward and join him.

"Your own Sue Pickering, who's playing our cousin, is having a birthday. She turned seventeen today. Would you all join me in singing 'Happy Birthday' to Sue?"

I gaze out over the sea of faces in the audience as their voices begin to rise. I am overwhelmed.

I think about Sonia guiding me into the living room, where all the girls clapped and cheered and sang "Happy Birthday." The coffee table held the biggest pile of presents I'd ever seen. Mom was smiling and holding out her arms to me. She was tan and so pretty in that rose-colored dress I liked so much. She looked so happy.

Victor Jory is right beside me singing and waving his arms as he leads the crowd in song. He looks just like a conductor. Hundreds of singing voices fill the giant room.

Happy birthday to you,
Happy birthday to you!

I am thrilled and, at the same time, I am embarrassed. I don't know where to look. I want to be gracious, but I'm so overwhelmed, it's hard to know what to do. Hundreds of people are singing happy birthday to me and Victor Jory is leading them! I take a quick look around for Jake. He's in the cast lineup, his eyes twinkling, his crooked smile stretched clear across his face. As I catch his eye, he raises his hand to me and makes a V, like a victory sign. I turn back to the front and grin at Mr. Jory, then I smile and nod at all those singing people out there. I clap my hands together and laugh out loud. I belong here.

WHAT'S NEXT

The visitor

I'm bundled up, wandering around the Home grounds. It's a cold, wet December day. What am I going to do after I graduate next month? Think, Susan, think, I tell myself.

"Sue?" It's Mac calling to me from his office window.

"Hi," I yell back. I'm kicking some snow along as I'm passing the Main Building. He looks out at me for a moment. He's not smiling.

"You want me to come up there?" I holler. He nods.

There's a man standing in Mac's office. His back is to me. He's dressed in some kind of military uniform. I stop inside the doorway. Maybe Mac's in the middle of something and I should wait. Besides, I'm wearing my old pea jacket and am not very "presentable," as Miss Maude would say.

The man turns around. It's Ronnie! Ronnie with the same beige glasses. Ronnie from two years ago. Ronnie from Florida.

What's he doing in Binghamton? Why is he here?

I look at him, but I don't say anything. I'm confused. Like when you're watching a program on TV and suddenly, when you look away for a minute, somebody changes the channel.

"Sue?" It's Mac talking. "Ronnie has asked to see you." Mac waits. We all wait.

"Hi Ronnie," I say. He smiles. He looks pretty much the same, but his hair is real short and he's older. Part of it's the uniform, I guess, but his eyes look tired, too. He's holding a cap in his hands.

"Hi." He looks over at Mac. "Is there someplace Sue and I can talk?"

Mac looks at me.

"There's a bench in the hallway," I say.

We start down the hall. We don't say anything. Why is he here, I wonder? When we reach the bench and sit down, I keep my eyes on the floor. Same old linoleum.

After a while, Ronnie says, "Mom says hi." I nod. "She sent you this." He pulls a small piece of white cloth out of his jacket pocket and unfolds it delicately, smoothing out the creases before he hands it to me. It's a handkerchief with lace around the edges. The material is soft and thin. His hands look rough and chapped, maybe from the cold.

"She made this for you. When I told her I was coming up to see you, she wanted me to bring it."

I take the hankie. "Tell her thank you. It's very pretty."

When he doesn't say anything more, I put the hankie in my pocket. Then I look at him. He's staring at me like he did in Florida.

"Why are you here?" I ask him. My voice sounds scratchy.

"I came to ask you something," he says.

I jam my fists deep into my coat pockets and tuck my head down.

"I'm in the military now, Sue. That means I'll be overseas for a while." He looks at me. "Maybe in Asia. Someplace over there."

It's like he isn't sure.

I'm restless, uncomfortable. The tip of my sneaker makes the same old squeaky noise on the linoleum.

"When I get back to the U.S., I was wondering . . . ." He stops. He wants me to jump in, to tell him I'll wait for him. Or something.

I glance at him. He's creasing the folds of his cap like he's ironing it with his fingers. I don't say anything.

He continues.

"Sue, will you write to me while I'm gone? And maybe, when I get back . . . ." His voice drifts off again.

Suddenly, my heart aches for him. I don't love him, but I don't want to hurt him either. Not after he was so crushed when I left him and Florida two and a half years ago.

"Ronnie?" My voice sounds gentle, which surprises me. "I can't tell you I'll wait for you. Or anything like that. It wouldn't be right. And besides, I'm only seventeen."

I feel stupid saying this, like being "too young" is my only excuse. But I don't want to talk about everything that's happened. It's none of his business that Peter is coming up from New York in January to take me to my senior prom. I don't want to talk about Peter. I don't want Ronnie to know anything about my life.

"I'm not ready to go steady." That sounds stupid even as I say it. But I don't know how else to describe what Ronnie wants from me. "And besides, we haven't even written since I was in Florida."

"I didn't want to bother you anymore," he says, looking down. He sounds serious.

If he knows that he bothered me that summer, when I had only just turned fifteen, why is he here now?

I take a deep breath.

"I'm really sorry you came all this way to see me. If I'd known about it, I would have asked you not to come."

I look up in time to see Mac duck back into his office.

I ask, "How did you get here anyway?"

"Greyhound," he says. He has an I-can't-believe-I-took-a-Greyhound expression. We both laugh.

"Wow. That's a long ride." He nods his head and smiles.

We make small talk for a while. His folks are fine. My aunt and uncle are fine. Yes, he finished college. Yes, I'm graduating from high school in a few weeks. Gradually, his shoulders drop down like he's starting to relax. Maybe it's easier for him, now that he knows for sure there's nothing between us. Or maybe he thinks there was something back in Florida and now it's over. Anyway, we stand and shake hands.

"Thank your mother for me," I tell him again. He looks puzzled. "For the hankie."

"Oh, yeah. She always liked you."

"I liked her, too." I don't remember her too clearly after all that we went through back then, but he doesn't need to know that.

I don't belong here

As soon as school lets out for the day, Betty, Bonnie and I cut across the half snowy, half muddy lawn and head for the Wigwam. We do this all the time now. And the two of them almost always talk about what's going to happen after our graduation in January. It's less than a month away.

"Do you know where you're going to go yet?" Bonnie asks Betty.

"I guess I'll start at Broome Community," Betty answers. "Then I'll transfer."

"Where to?"

She shrugs. "Harpur College, I guess. Mom says it's pretty good."

It's usually Betty who asks, "Where are you going to go, Sue?" Now it's my turn to shrug. I'm too embarrassed to tell them I haven't even applied. I've got the grades, but I don't have the money. And I don't know how to get any money. When I went to see the counselor about going to college, she looked me over and said, "You live at the Home. Am I correct?" I nodded. Then she added, "Well, I guess you better find a job."

Now it's already the new year, and we're getting ready to graduate. I don't know what else to do, so I go see the counselor again. Not about school, but about finding that job.

She runs her finger down my transcript. "So. I see you took four years of Latin and four years of French. That's impressive." She doesn't sound impressed at all.

"Almost all college prep courses. That's pretty unusual in a vocational high school." She stares at me for a moment, her eyebrows raised.

I'm embarrassed, like I've come in the door marked Exit. Most of the kids at North High take Welding or Beginning Clerical Skills or Home Economics. I thought my college prep courses would be my way out. But I don't know how to make that happen. I'm afraid to go to Mac or Miss Maude about it. Their job is done. I'm the first kid from the Home to graduate from high school. How can I ask them for anything more?

"No college plans, I take it," the counselor says. It's not a question.

"No money," I tell her.

She checks the time on the wall clock that's behind me. I clear my throat.

"I need to get a job."

"Excuse me?"

I raise my voice. "Can you help me find a job?"

She shuffles papers.

"What kind of work experience have you had?"

Now I really don't dare look at her.

"I was an apprentice in the theater last summer. I built sets and worked backstage and played some bit parts."

When I raise my eyes, she is looking at me in disbelief.

"Not a very practical choice for a girl in your situation, would you say?"

Her eyes are distant. I am silent.

"Well, I certainly hope you found the time to take Typing, Sue."

I exhale. Finally, I have the right answer. "Yes. And I got an A."

She rustles through more papers, then holds one up. "Here's a really good job for you. Accounts Receivable Clerk at Ozalid film factory." She's got a thin smile now. "Lots of our girls go to work there. At least until they get married and start a family." She looks at me over the rim of her glasses like she's estimating how long I'll need that job. I think of Ronnie and my stomach ties up in a knot.

She hands me a slip of paper with the factory's address. "Here's where you go to apply. Good luck, Sue."

Welcome to Ozalid

Factories scare me. Even though I work in the office at Ozalid, it's still a factory. When I was little, I watched my mom get sick and collapse when she worked on the line in a shoe factory. It's only been a few weeks, but I need to get out of here. I don't want anything to do with factories.

When break time is over, I grind out my cigarette and head back toward my desk. Women move through the aisles, brushing doughnut crumbs from their blouses and tucking cigarette packs in their purses. They laugh together. They are comfortable here.

I want to yell and bang on their desks as I pass. I want to tell these women, "I don't belong here."

I walk slowly, eyes down. I need to let my mind float. Hold myself together. Don't talk.

I want something more than being an Accounts Receivable Clerk in a factory, something out there, something that is so hard to define it makes my head hurt.

"Sue?"

A blond girl is standing in front of my desk. Her name is Fay. She looks down at me through her lashes in a way that tells me she hardly sees me.

"Are you still taking the bus to work?" she asks. She plays with the ends of her blond wavy hair. Her dress is flashy.

I nod. I look down at my desk. I hate the long bus ride.

"We could ride together, if you want. I have a car now." I've seen her car. It's turquoise with lots of chrome. I think about it.

Don't become one of them, I warn myself. If you step into their world, your dreams will disappear.

"It's too far. I come all the way from the other side of Binghamton," I announce, like that's the end of the conversation.

"I know. I've seen you at the bus stop. I go right past there every day. Conklin Avenue, right?"

"Right." I look up at her, surprised.

"If you could help me out with gas money," she says, "you'd get here sooner and you wouldn't have to ride that jerky bus." She laughs.

It sounds good, but I'm not sure. Fay has what Miss Maude would call a "fast look" that makes me uneasy. Then I think about the long dreary bus rides and the smell of diesel exhaust.

"Could we try it for a week?" I ask. She nods. I can see by her grin she's already planning how to spend the extra gas money.

We start our arrangement on Monday. I get to ride in Fay's car, and she gets a captive audience for her stories. It doesn't take long for me to figure out that I'm riding in silence in a warm car so I can go to a job I don't want in a place where I don't belong.

Travels with Fay

It's the morning of our third day driving to and from Ozalid together. Fay is talking, as usual, and "Mr. Sandman" is playing on the radio. Fay talks a lot about where the cool kids are hanging out. This month it's at a drive-in bar-be-cue called Pigs-something-or-other. I don't catch the whole name.

"It's so cool, Sue. The waitresses come out to your car on roller skates."

I have a sudden vision of Fay skating out to a car, carrying a tray of burgers and shakes and wearing what looks like a cheer-leader costume. Glancing over at her wavy blond hair and listening to her bouncy voice, I can see she'd be good at it.

I don't say much on our drives. Fay doesn't really want to hear from me anyway. She's off in her own dreamland.

Fay is talking pretty fast when she drives right through the stop sign. As we swing into the intersection, a car slams into my door. With my heart pounding, I turn and look out my window. There's a startled gray-haired man wearing an overcoat behind the wheel.

We aren't hurt, and Fay tells me later that day that the insurance company will pay for the big dent in the door. We continue going to work together, and after the trial week is up, I agree to keep riding with her.

It isn't long—just a few weeks—before we are in another accident. Fay is talking, as usual, when it happens. This time a tall woman with dark brown too-curly hair gets out of her car right after we hit her and begins smacking my window with her purse.

"What on earth are you two doing?" she yells through the glass.

Fay shrugs as though these things happen every day, which seems like it's almost true.

"Fay, what do I say to her?" I ask.

"Tell her I was busy."

Two accidents in a month. Riding with Fay is not good for my health. Neither is working in this factory.

The big move

Not long after the second accident, I bump the last cardboard box down the cottage stairs and drag it into the Staff Room. That's what they call the extra bedroom next to the kitchen that the substitute housemothers use when they stay over. But now, according to Miss Maude, it's going to be my room!

I flip on the overhead light and look around. There's a single bed and a dresser stained a shade of orange that's so bright it makes me squint. I salute myself in the mirror over the dresser. Here's to the high school graduate who has a job, awful as it is, and her own room.

The wheels in my head start to spin. What if, when I turn eighteen, I have to leave here and go . . . I don't know where. I sit down on the bed. The older kids talk all the time about what happens when you "age out." Your eighteenth birthday comes and, overnight—*wham*—you're out of foster care. You're all alone, no money, no home, no anything. I take a deep breath and tell myself not to think about that right now. Almost six more months, I tell myself, until that day comes. I look around my room and mumble a tiny thank you prayer for getting this far.

I tuck my very new Binghamton North High School Diploma in the corner of the mirror. Mac and Miss Maude are so proud of it—of me, I guess—and I am, too. They remind me all the time that it means a lot for a Home kid to graduate.

As I wash my hands in the fake marble bathroom sink, I hear myself humming. Having my own room and bath feels so good. No more fighting for a dry towel, hands dripping on the floor. No more jiggling, legs crossed, waiting for a toilet stall. I touch the shower curtain. Yes! The shower curtain is made of cloth. No more rubbery vinyl.

I unpack my high school textbooks and prop them in a row across the back of the small desk. Latin. French. Algebra. Geometry. All those college prep courses. I am proud I took those courses and passed all the New York State Regents exams. But will I ever go somewhere, *do* something? Just thinking about whether I can ever get to go to college makes me tense up all over.

Soon after I get my first paycheck, I go straight to the bank and open an account. Mac wants to drive me, but I tell him I'll take the bus. I don't want to look like a kid who needs to be carted around.

"Can I help you?" The bank teller isn't much older than I am. She glances at me in my scruffy wool scarf and unfashionable pea jacket and suddenly finds something behind the bank counter very interesting.

"I'm here to open an account." I keep my voice steady.

"A checking account?" Her voice is snooty and matches her bangs, which are way fluffed up in front. I bet she uses those huge pink rollers they sell at Woolworths.

"No," I tell her. "Savings." Right away, I know this is the wrong answer. Adults have checking accounts, her raised eyebrows tell me. Kids have savings accounts. I am growing warm under my collar.

"Are you eighteen yet?" she asks, peering at me over the edge of the counter. I want to ask her if she's eighteen yet, but I know Miss Maude would consider that a "fresh remark."

"I'm seventeen," I answer. "I'll be eighteen in July." That's almost six months away, but it's the best I can do. "I've already graduated from high school. And I have a job." I stand up straight and push my paycheck across the counter. She is not the only one working.

She barely looks at my paycheck before waving me off to an older woman who kindly offers me a chair across from her desk. In a quiet voice, this woman helps me fill in the forms. She looks as though she's happy to have me in their bank.

By the time I'm on the bus going home, I have my very own savings account booklet in the name of Susan DuMond Pickering tucked into my purse, right next to my Pall Malls.

MAKING IT HAPPEN

Mac's idea

Each night when I get home from the factory, I open the door to my little room and give my "warm and safe" sigh. Tonight, I take off my pea jacket and wave to the "handsome couple" (Miss Maude's phrase) in the prom picture hanging on my wall.

That night in January, when we climbed out of Peter's car at the senior prom, I bet people thought we were chaperones. Peter's in his twenties, which is something we didn't talk about very much. His dark, slender look is perfect for a tuxedo. Mac and Miss Maude agreed I could have a brand new, all-my-own dress. It's turquoise, with just the right amount of netting, and it's strapless, with tiny soft turquoise feathers around the edge of the top.

Peter was so sweet to come all the way from New York, even though we both knew we were coming to an end. I already knew his parents were giving him a hard time—what's a twenty-something doing dating a seventeen-year-old who lives in a children's home, for God's sake? And when I found out his father was an important lawyer or a judge or something, I knew we were doomed. But we had our prom night. Dancing, floating, flowers on my wrist, and the band playing "Earth Angel."

I pat the prom picture, then I check the due dates on the library books I've added to my textbook collection. Next I straighten the pillow Miss Maude gave me to brighten things up a bit. It has wavy blue and green lines that remind me of the ocean.

I am on my way out of the bathroom after my shower when I hear a gentle knock on the door.

"Coming," I holler, thinking it's probably Miss Maude. Wrapped in my oversized faded flannel robe with a towel twisted around my wet hair, I swing the door open. Oh geez, it's Mac! I blush, but he doesn't seem to notice or care how I look.

"How's work?" he asks as he walks by me. It sounds a lot like "How's school?" which used to be his favorite question.

It's a snowy evening in February. His cheeks are red from the cold, and his thin hair is pointing in all directions. He's tucked the ends of his red plaid scarf into his gray tweed jacket. He wears the scarf all the time, telling anyone who will listen that it keeps him in touch with his Scottish heritage.

My room doesn't have a whole lot of places to sit, which I didn't even think about until Mac showed up. He heads straight for my only chair, pulling it away from the writing desk and turning it to face the bed. I sit down on the edge of the bed.

"Work's okay. I've pretty much learned everything I need to know to be an accounts receivable clerk." I shrug. "I guess I'm doing okay."

He nods. "Not too exciting, is it?"

"It's a paycheck." I look away in surprise. My mother must have said this a hundred times whenever someone asked her how she liked whatever job she was doing at the moment. It makes me squirm to think I'm already thinking of my job as a "paycheck."

Mac shifts in the little chair, loosening his scarf. He turns toward me.

"Sue, I've been thinking."

I smile, but it's a small smile. I've heard Mac say that often enough over the years. Most of the time it means something unusual or unexpected is about to happen, like the time I ended up in Florida with my aunt and uncle.

"Thinking about what?" I ask.

"About college."

Of all things, I hiccup. I guess my body volunteers it out of surprise.

"What about college?" He doesn't answer right away. "Mac, are you thinking about *me* going to college?"

When Mac smiles, it's like God or the electric company turns on a special light bulb inside his head. A warm golden glow fills the room. I can't help smiling back at him as he grins at me. His bright blue eyes still have that bit of a Santa Claus twinkle.

"And why not, Miss Pickering?" he asks. "You're now a high school graduate." I glance at the diploma tucked into my dresser mirror. I've heard often enough how I am the first Home kid to finish high school.

I stand up, suddenly feeling like I ought to close the bathroom door. It doesn't seem right to be having this important conversation with the door to the bathroom wide open and the steam from my shower drifting into the bedroom.

I shut the door and turn back to face Mac.

"College costs a lot of money. A whole lot. Even with my job at the factory, there's no way I can save enough to go to college."

I think about the fifty-two dollars I've managed to save, scrubbing floors and cooking breakfasts for the girls in my cottage. Geez, that probably isn't even enough for a bus ticket to get me out of town.

Mac watches as I cross my arms and shake my head.

"Sue," he says. He's serious now. "You deserve to go to college. And I deserve to have you go, too." I'm not sure what he means by that. "I think, if we put our heads together, we can do it. But only if you're willing."

I sit down again on the edge of the bed and take a deep breath. I figure if I say no, Mac will be back in a few days and we'll be having this conversation all over again. He is that stubborn. He says that's part of being Scottish. And in my secret heart, I want to go to college so very much. So I put my toe in the water. I lean forward.

"What do I have to do?"

"Go visit your high school counselor."

I pull back and make a face.

"Now, Sue, I know you don't like her. And I know you've already graduated. But she'll have catalogs and brochures, and you can begin to see what's out there."

"She never liked me," I mumble. "She thinks I took all the wrong courses for a Home girl."

"We need to move fast," he adds, ignoring my comment. "Sue, it's probably my fault we didn't get this started long before you graduated. I'm truly sorry about that." There is such kindness in his eyes, I find myself wondering if this is what it is like to have a father. "I should have realized sooner," he says.

"Realized what?"

"That you're smart and special." He glances down at the carpet. "And," he adds, "that you're dripping water on the floor."

Fredonia

"Mac? It's me, Sue." I'm hopping from one foot to the other to keep warm. There isn't any door on the phone booth. There's ice on the panes of glass that aren't broken. I make a frosty cloud every time I exhale.

"Sue!" He sounds startled. I hardly ever call him. "Are you all right? Where are you?"

"I'm at the high school."

"The high school? What are you doing at the high school?"

"I went to see the guidance counselor like you said. I wanted to look at some college catalogs."

"That's great! What did you find out?"

"She thinks I should keep my job at the factory. She thinks I'm lucky to have it." Silence. "She says I probably couldn't get a scholarship now anyway. It's too late."

It's beginning to snow. More silence from Mac.

"She gave me a booklet for one college, though. But they don't have any theater courses."

"Theater courses?" Mac sounds like this idea is coming from outer space.

"Well, I've been thinking about it. After being an apprentice last summer and being in plays in high school, I'm pretty sure that's what I want to study." He doesn't say anything. "Anyway, I have the application. But I don't think it's the right school for me."

"What school is it?" he asks.

I reach into my pocket and pull out the wrinkled brochure.

"It's called Fredonia State Teachers College. Do you know where it is?"

"Yes, Sue," he answers patiently. "It's in Fredonia."

I roll my eyes.

"Did you tell her you want to be a teacher?" he asks.

"No, I did not. I told her I want to be an actress. Or maybe a director. But I definitely did *not* tell her I want to be a teacher. That was her idea."

By now, I'm stamping my feet like mad to keep from freezing.

"Well, it's not such a bad idea. Is there any way we can interest you in it?"

I stop stamping. I don't answer.

Instead I tell him, "I did find another school though. Wait till you hear about it. It's a girls' school and it's near New York City. It's called Sarah Lawrence."

I hear a groan.

"Sue, do you have any idea how much Sarah Lawrence costs?" It's his serious voice.

"No." I sigh. "But it sounds like you do."

He laughs.

"Get on the bus and come home. If you catch pneumonia out there, Miss Maude will have my hide." Then he adds, "I'm sorry the counselor wasn't much help."

"Hey, Mac, I'm a 'Home kid.' And even Home kids who get A's in Latin and French don't go to college. We all know that."

Now we are both laughing.

"Sue, dear, I'll say this. For a Home kid, you have great taste in colleges."

One door closes, another opens

My head is going in a million directions. Mac called Sarah Lawrence College and, after they talked for a long time, they asked us to come to the school so I could apply in person. In a week! They told him I could bring all the papers I need with me. I worked like mad, writing and rewriting my essay, especially the part about Mom, and filling in the application they sent. And now I keep worrying that I've forgotten something important.

We've been at Sarah Lawrence for two days, and Mac and I are sitting across the desk from an admissions officer. I've been interviewed by all sorts of people, and I've seen every corner of this very ritzy campus. I keep waiting for someone to point at me and yell, "You're a Home girl! You don't belong here!"

The lady speaks in a quiet voice. "Everything we've seen suggests you'll do very well in college, Sue." Then she frowns and looks out the window.

Here it comes.

"We're just not sure Sarah Lawrence is the right place for you."

I've spent hours answering embarrassing questions, acting confident, telling my I-was-taken-to-the-Home story over and over again. And now this.

"Not the right place?" Mac sounds like he didn't quite hear her correctly.

I drop my eyes. I'm so embarrassed, I almost miss her reply.

"Unfortunately, we don't have a great many scholarships." She gestures toward the window. "You may have noticed the expensive cars in the parking lot." Mac nods. "Most of our students come from very wealthy families. Obviously Sue does not have that advantage." She says this matter of fact, like a weather report. "We believe she will do better where she doesn't have the social pressure she'd find here."

I look around her office at the tall bookcases, the drapes, the shiny paperweight with her initials on it. Everything looks like it costs a lot of money.

She's talking to me now.

"Sue, you're certainly bright enough. And you deserve a chance." She studies me. "I've talked this over with some of the staff. We think the best place for you would be Bennington College, another fine school."

She waits. Mac and I don't say anything.

"Are you familiar with Bennington?"

I shake my head. I want to sneak out of here and forget the whole thing.

"It's a very good school. It's in Vermont." She takes a deep breath. "And they have more scholarships than we do." She looks me in the eye. "Sue, they have a fine theater department. You'd do well to go there." She folds her hands and rests them on the edge of her desk. Her nails are perfect.

I turn to Mac. "Do you know about Bennington?"

"I've heard of it, yes," he nods. He straightens his tie and turns to face the Sarah Lawrence woman. "Well, what are our next steps?"

Our next steps? Wow.

"I'd like to call them," she answers. Then she turns to me. "I'd like to recommend you, Sue, if that would be all right. I truly think Bennington would be the perfect place for you." She smiles.

I stare at her. Is it possible Bennington would want me?

"Plus," she adds, "it's already March, and we're trying to get you enrolled for September. That's not exactly easy." She rises from her chair. "If you'll give me a few minutes, perhaps I can reach them and have some information for you."

Mac and I stand. "We'll be in the hall," he tells her. He touches my arm, and I follow him out into the hallway.

We wait in silence. He looks out the hallway window. I stare at a rack of colorful brochures. I feel like my mind is frozen. After a while, I feel his hand on my shoulder. "We'll make it, Sue. Honest to God, we're going to find the right school." I turn to face him. "The right school for you." I'm trying to hold the pieces together, and he can tell.

The door opens.

"Well! Bennington is very interested," she announces with what looks like a genuine smile. "They'd like to see you next week-end. They're sending you an application today." She gives a little clap. "I hope you don't mind taking another long drive in the snow." Mac glances at me. I see a grin starting.

She pulls a map from her desk drawer and spreads it out so we can see where Bennington is. She and Mac talk about the best route to get there from Binghamton. I watch her write down directions and names.

When she hands the paper to Mac, a tiny part of me starts to get excited. A bigger part feels like I'm standing at the bottom of a very deep hole.

No guts, no glory

The long driveway is lined on both sides with tall snowy trees. It goes on forever. Still no buildings.

"Where is the school?"

My stomach is doing flip-flops and my heart is pumping a lot faster than Mac is driving. Bennington could be my chance. My *only* chance.

"Take it easy, kiddo. The campus covers hundreds of acres. We have a ways to go yet."

Why was the woman at Sarah Lawrence so sure I belonged here? Even the lettering on the Bennington College sign where we turned in looked elegant. If it weren't for Mac, I'd be on the next Greyhound bus back to ordinary old Binghamton. I lean my head back and close my eyes.

When I was eleven, before I was sent to the Home, I loved to go skating with my friend, Henry. After school, I would sit on the curb and wait for him. We'd skate down what we called "Cocktail Hill." We called it that because, halfway down, there was a sign that blinked "Cocktail Lounge." It had a funny-looking glass with an olive in it that made us laugh. The hill lasted for one really long block. The street was lined with boarded-up buildings. Toward the bottom, there were piles of old cars behind a sign that read "Engine Parts Sold Cheap."

As soon as Henry showed up, we'd put on our skates.

"Hey Sue. Want me to tighten yours?"

"Nah. I'm okay." I used to twist the key so hard, the metal would pinch my shoes. I didn't want them to come loose. Just in case, I always wore long pants.

Henry and I would stand on the sidewalk at the top of the hill watching the traffic. We wanted to be sure no cars were turning onto the cross street at the bottom when we did a "hit and run."

To do a good "hit and run," you pushed off hard at the top of the hill. You crouched down and pulled your arms in close. Sometimes you'd go so fast your eyes would water and everything looked blurry. You'd sail past the cocktail sign and the car parts and then, POW, you'd fly off the curb, bounce once in the middle of the street—that was the "hit"—and land on the sidewalk where it gets flat so you could coast to a stop—that was the "run." Each of us did the "hit and run" separately. The other one watched for traffic.

When I open my eyes, Mac is pulling into a big, nearly empty parking lot. The one car I see is under inches of snow. I'm glad I wore my boots.

At the edge of the lot, Mac stops and unfolds the directions.

"We're looking for a building called The Barn," he tells me. "Let's try this way." We stomp off through the snow.

We round a corner and stop. The building in front of us is wooden and it's painted red. The bright color makes it look sort of like a barn.

"This must be it," he says. He gives my arm a quick squeeze and we pick a door.

The hall is empty. We walk toward a sign that says, "Admissions Office." Inside, there's a waiting room with chairs and a table with a handful of magazines and a stack of Bennington College catalogs. A man comes out of his office to meet us.

"You must be Sue Pickering," he says. He's smiling. His handshake is strong.

He turns to Mac. "And I presume you're John McPherson." His voice is deep and sort of relaxed, like he's not in a hurry. Kind of like Mac.

He introduces himself as the Admissions Director, and the three of us go into his office, where we talk for a long time. He wants to know all about me, like they did at Sarah Lawrence.

"Was it hard for you, Sue, living in the Home?"

I look over at Mac. He wants to hear my answer, too.

"Before Miss Maude came—she's my housemother—it was pretty hard." I glance at Mac again. "Some kids—quite a few—got sent to reform school." Pause. "But Miss Maude takes good care of me. Of us. And Mac's always there to help." I feel lame, like I'm missing the important parts, and I don't even know what they are. It's like trying to put a puzzle together without ever seeing the picture.

After a while, the man asks why I went to a vocational high school.

"I didn't choose it. It's where all of us who live at the Home go." He nods. "But I was able to take college prep courses."

"And your record shows you did very well," he says. I drop my gaze. I would have worked a lot harder if I thought I'd ever get to go to college.

Then Mac steps in. "Sue is the first resident of the Home to graduate from high school in our hundred-year history. She's an honor graduate. And she's done a lot of good work in our summer stock theater."

The Admissions Director leans forward. "Tell me about your experience in the theater, Sue."

So I do. I tell him about building a new set every week, working side by side with the House Carpenter. And how Arthur Treacher taught me what a Dutchman is. I talk about how much I learned being on stage with Victor Jory, and about how he led the audience in singing "Happy Birthday" to me. And about how I was responsible for shepherding Tallulah Bankhead on stage for every performance.

He's laughing now, enjoying the stories.

Mac looks at me. "Needless to say, we're all proud of Sue and what she's accomplished."

We talk some more. I don't say anything about Mom, and the Admissions Director doesn't ask.

Finally, the man starts talking about Bennington. "We keep our enrollment small," he says. "We have about three hundred girls here. And it feels like we have just as many faculty!" Mac laughs. I guess it's a joke.

"You'd have lots of opportunities here, Sue," the Director says. "We have really fine teachers. Small classes. And, believe me, our theater department is top notch." I smile.

"But it could also be a big challenge for you, after your years in the Home." He's studying me, wondering if I can do it. I'm wondering, too.

"Where are all the students?" I ask, to break the silence.

"Bennington students work off-campus for a few months every winter. It's called Non-Resident Term. Some go to Europe or the Far East to do volunteer work in their field." He looks at me. "But lots of girls take jobs that will give them good experience and help pay the bills."

When we return to the waiting room, there's a girl sitting there. She has on a big parka, heavy lace-up boots, and a wool hat that covers the top of her long dark hair. "Oh good, you're here," says the Director. "This is Rachel. She'll be showing you the campus." He turns to me. "Rachel's working with us for her Non-Resident Term."

More hand shaking.

"Make sure Sue and Mr. McPherson get a good look at the theater. Sue's interested in our Drama program."

"Okay," the girl answers. She turns to me. "I'm a music major. Piano. I'm going to be a composer."

Wow.

Mac, Rachel, and I walk for what seems like miles. Sometimes we talk; sometimes we listen to our boots squeak on the snow. We tour classrooms, a sculpture studio, the library. Later on, she tells me, we'll go inside one of the houses where the girls live.

"Now let's go see the theater."

We walk into a large, three-story brick building with a wooden second-story balcony that's painted white. Rachel tells us the theater is on the top floor. As we go in, we pass a snack bar. The tables and chairs are empty. Rachel points to a sign for the infirmary, which is also on the first floor.

A flight of wide stairs leads to the kitchen and dining rooms. "You can wait tables here, if you need a job," Rachel tells me. "I do it. And Mike's great. He runs the kitchen."

Need a job? You bet!

"Once when I was in the infirmary, Mike sent down a bowl of tomato soup and then a double scoop of chocolate ice cream. It made me feel better right away, you know?"

We laugh. Mac shakes his head.

Looking out over the balcony from the dining room window, there's a long open space that's probably a lawn. It's bordered on two sides by large white houses. "Those are the dorms, where we live," Rachel says. "There are more houses like these, but you can't see them from here."

At the end of the snow-covered lawn, there's a wall. Rachel sees me looking.

"That's where we sit and read and hang out when the weather's nice. It's an old stone wall. We call it the end of the world."

We leave the dining room and walk up the last flight of stairs to the theater.

When I step inside, it feels like I'm back at the summer stock theater. It's not fancy, but it's solid and warm, a good place to be. Rachel and Mac sit down in the front row. I'm already heading for the stairs that lead to the stage.

"Is it all right if I go backstage?"

Rachel nods. "We'll wait here."

I disappear into the wings and find my way to the back of the theater. Backstage is cool and dark, and it smells a little dusty. I find an open dressing room. A long skirt that looks like part of a costume hangs from a hook on the wall. There's a faint smell of makeup. I start back toward the stage and stop for a moment in the wings. I have that butterfly feeling, like I'm about to make my entrance.

"Sue? Ready to move on?" It's Mac.

"Coming." I cross my fingers for good luck, just like I used to do years ago. Soon I join Mac and Rachel out front, and we leave the theater.

We walk through more snow for what feels like another mile to Jennings Hall. Our guide's excited. It's the music building. "I practically live here!" she tells us.

Jennings is a large stone building facing a meadow. It looks like the manor house in a story. Inside, the three of us sit on a wooden bench in the hallway. Someone is playing the cello. "Who's that?" I ask Rachel.

"It's George Finkel," she tells us. "His studio is in Jennings. He's pretty well-known." I can tell she's really proud.

I close my eyes and listen to the sound travel through this old stone building with the high ceilings. I think about learning to play the cello in the sixth grade and how I loved the sound. I feel I am either going to go right to sleep or I am going to cry.

After two days of examining every corner of the campus and talking to practically every teacher and staff member who's around, we're back in the Admissions Office. I'm tired and wary. It's decision time. I stare at the wet marks my boots left on the floor.

That's when I hear the Director say, "Sue, Bennington would like to have you start as a freshman in September." I look in his eyes to see if there is truth there.

"But, as you know, scholarships have already been handed out for the fall."

I knew it. I start to button my jacket.

"However, we're going to look very hard to see if we can come up with half the money. We'll need to be very creative at this point in the year. But I think we can do it." He looks at me, then at Mac. "The rest will be up to you."

Nobody says anything.

"Is that acceptable?" he asks.

Mac and I lock eyes. We had read about how Bennington is one of the most expensive colleges in the nation. But now, here's my chance. It's too good to turn down, but how will I ever pay for it? While Mac and the Director talk about tuition, the cost of housing, and how much I could make working in the dining hall, I walk over to the window and stare out at the snow.

I think about one of the times it was my turn to do a "hit and run" and Henry was the lookout. We watched a car pass us and drive down the hill. As soon as the road was clear, Henry waved and I took off, legs pumping, feet flying. I was going so fast I skimmed over the cracks and bumps in the sidewalk. Buildings were a blur. I pulled my arms in tight and bent down low. That's when I heard a car turn onto Cocktail Hill behind me. I skated hard and fast. I heard Henry yelling, but I didn't stop.

At the bottom, I shot off the end of the sidewalk and went straight up into the air like a cannonball. I flew so fast I sailed right over the "hit" mark. With my heart racing, I heard a car turn into the street right behind me as I landed on the sidewalk and finally coasted to a stop. It was the first time one of us cleared the street without a "hit."

Later that day, as we were walking home, I noticed Henry looking at me.

"Know what you are, Sue?" he asked. "You're the Queen of Cocktail Hill."

Remembering my victory, my surviving, my being called a queen, I turn away from the window and walk across the room to stand at Mac's side.

"Well, what do you think, Sue?" the Director asks.

"Thank you," I tell him, my voice strong. "Thank you very much. I'd be happy to come to Bennington."

We all shake hands, smiling, talking over each other's sentences.

Our drive home on Sunday is quiet. We're tired and relieved. I am partway between dreamland and a good case of the nerves, as Miss Maude would say. I hope the Admissions Director is right in trying to find scholarship money for a girl who lives in a children's home, who graduated from a vocational high school, and who works in a factory.

"Sue? Are you asleep?"

I keep my eyes closed and shake my head no.

"How did you like Bennington?" he asks for maybe the tenth time as we travel toward home.

"I liked it. A lot. But it's going to cost so much." I look over at Mac. "How are we going to get our half together by September?" I count on my fingers. "That's less than six months."

"Well," he answers, "I suppose we could rob a bank."

I crack up. Then I close my eyes again.

"Mac? Which house do you think I'll get to live in?"

"Which one would you like?"

"I'd like one that's way at the end of the road, down by the end of the world."

A windfall

It's the next morning. I'm exhausted, and the adrenaline is still pumping. I'm standing in winter slush on Conklin Avenue, waiting for Fay to pick me up for work. I know it would be smart to stop riding with her after the accidents, but right now I'm too worried about money to deal with the bus. Under my breath, I repeat, "This will all be over in six months. This will all be over in six months."

Our drive is quiet. Fay must have had a big weekend. She looks tired, and she doesn't have any makeup on yet. She doesn't say much, which is okay with me. I don't say anything about visiting Bennington or about maybe going away to school in the fall. I don't want anyone at the factory to know yet. If they knew I was hoping and planning to leave, it could cost me my job.

That night the phone rings in the upstairs hall.

I hear Miss Maude call down the stairs. "Sue, it's for you."

Just out of the shower, I grab my robe and wrap a towel around my head. As I take the stairs two at a time, I wonder whether it's Peter. Maybe we're not really broken up after all.

"Hello?"

"Is this Sue Pickering?"

It's a man, but it's not Peter.

"Yes?"

"Miss Pickering, do you work at Ozalid factory?"

"Yes, I do."

"And do you normally ride to work with Miss Fay Connors?"

Oh geez. It's about the accidents.

"Uh huh."

I want to tell him I'm not going to ride with Fay any more, but he's already talking.

"Uh, Miss Pickering." He clears his throat. "I represent Miss Connors' insurance company. As you might imagine, we're somewhat concerned about your safety. It's not that Miss Connors is not a good driver . . . ."

His voice is too smooth. I don't trust it. He waits for me to say something. I don't.

" . . . however we do think it's unusual for her to have had two accidents in such a short period of time."

I still don't say anything.

"Miss Pickering?"

"I'm here."

"Would you consider not riding to work anymore with Miss Connors? Would that be a possibility?"

"Uh, do you mean taking the bus again? Is that what you mean?"

"Yes, well, we realize that's an inconvenience, Miss Pickering. And we're prepared to, uh, reimburse you for that inconvenience."

Reimburse me for that inconvenience? Wow! And here I am, about to go back to the bus so I won't be killed!

I sigh. I know I have to tell him.

"Well, just so you know," I say, "I'd already pretty much decided to take the bus from now on. So I guess you don't need to 'reimburse' me."

It feels good to be honest, but having a little extra money right now would have been a really good thing.

"We certainly understand, Miss Pickering. However, in return for your taking the bus and, uh, signing a release saying you were not harmed during either of the two accidents, we are prepared to present you with a check for, say, one thousand dollars."

I get really quiet.

That's a lot of money. I don't want to say anything to make his offer go away. This could make a big difference in my not-yet-started Bennington fund. A really big difference. But I don't want to take it if it's wrong somehow.

"I think I'd better talk this over with my guardian," I tell him. "Would that be okay?"

"Of course," he says. He's sounding a bit more jovial now. "You're not yet eighteen, is that correct? Why don't you and he talk it over, and he can give me a call. We want to do what's right and reimburse you for your inconvenience."

"So, Mac, that's what the man said," I explain out of breath. I'm afraid Mac will say I have to turn down the thousand dollars.

"You didn't ask him for any money?"

"No, sir. I wouldn't do that," I say, surprised Mac would even think that.

He nods. He's thinking it over.

"Well, Miss Pickering, are you prepared to ride the bus to work until you leave for Bennington in the fall?"

"Oh boy, am I!"

Maybe he thinks it's okay to accept the money. Just maybe.

"And you haven't been hurt in any way during these accidents? We don't need any injuries coming back to haunt us, you know."

I shake my head. The accidents dented the door on my side both times, but that was it.

"Well, let's make sure this insurance fellow understands that there's no real reason to give you this money. But if he still insists, well, darn it, we'll take it. It will help a lot, come September."

I exhale.

The package

I lean against the heavy door to the Main Building and shake the water off my boots. It's a rainy Saturday afternoon. Mac left word with Miss Maude that the postman had delivered a package for me, and it's waiting for me in his office.

I've never gotten a package in the mail before. "Come and see, Sue," he says when I call to ask him what it is. "It's not a two-headed snake, I can guarantee you that."

Mac's office is small, but it always impresses me. I love the big wooden teacher's desk and the tall, overflowing bookcases. Today I notice more gray in his hair and the circles under his eyes seem deeper.

"Come in, come in," he says, pointing toward the visitor's chair.

The package on the corner of his desk is about twice as big as a deck of cards. There's heavy twine wrapped around the brown paper.

Mac nudges the package toward me. I pick it up. The paper is wrinkled and soiled in spots, like it has had a hard journey. The knot is tight. The black lettering is upright and strong. There's my name.

Sue Pickering
c/o Susquehanna Valley Home
100 Home Avenue
Binghamton, New York

My mind starts churning. I am afraid to ask, but I do anyway. "Is this from my father?"

I think about the photograph where he's holding me when I was a baby. I wonder now, as I always do, why he went away back then. And then I wonder why I think this package might be from him.

Mac leans back in his chair, watching. "Why don't you open it?"

He hands me a pair of scissors and I cut the twine. Underneath is a small dark spot, like someone spilled a drop of coffee. And here's a tiny rip, maybe from meeting up with a sharp corner.

"I got a robe from him once. I think I was seven." My voice is low. "It was yellow and had little trains on it. My name was embroidered on the trains in red."

I am confused. And I am afraid.

I slide my thumb under the tape and separate the edges of the brown paper. Inside there is more paper. It's covered with gold and silver stripes and what is now a flat gold bow. It's fancy.

Somebody tucked a small envelope under the bow. It has my name on it. I stare at it for a while, then I slide it out and open it. Inside is a heavy cream-colored card. It feels like velvet. I open the card.

"Susan, Congratulations on your graduation. Love, Dad"

The S in my name is tall and straight.

Mac rises from his chair and looks out the window. Rain makes streaks on the glass. The light outside is almost gone. We're in shadow.

I stare at the gold and silver paper until I can't stand it anymore. I try not to tear it when I open the box. Inside is a delicate gold watch with a round face and thin black numbers.

I rest the box with the watch still inside on the edge of Mac's desk.

"How did he find out?"

Mac's back is to the window now. It's so dark in the room, I can barely make out his features. "I wrote to him," he tells me.

"But I graduated in January. It's almost *summer* now." I lower my head and blink away the tears.

"I'm sorry, Sue. Sometimes things take longer than we like."

I want to take the watch out but I just look at it. After a while, I gather it up in its box along with all the paper and stand up, pulling on my coat.

"I didn't mean to upset you, Sue. Maybe I should have left well enough alone."

I shake my head no. I gather my father's gift and walk out the door.

Passing the hat

The toes of my patent leather pumps are scuffed and there's a run in my stocking. I'm sitting on a folding chair on a tiny stage to the right of the podium where Mac is speaking. The lights are hot and bright. The dampness under my arms is spreading.

"Sue has done exceptional work as a student, and she's a fine young woman. She graduated from North High this January with honors." Mac glances down at me. "She had the temerity to apply to college and, I am proud to announce, she has been accepted at Bennington College, a very fine school in Vermont."

Scattered applause. Strangers in a meeting hall in a factory town in upstate New York are staring at me because I need money to go to a school in Vermont they never heard of.

If I live through this, I swear I'll never again ask people for money.

"And now, I am proud to introduce Sue Pickering, who will share her story with you."

Mac and I exchange places. I rise and grip the edges of the podium. He sits on the little folding chair, looking up at me expectantly. Without even a glance, I know he is smiling and proud. We have done this six times so far.

I tell my story, but it's not the whole story. I don't say very much about Mom. Mac agreed I could leave out the hard parts.

My unblinking eyes roam the audience as I talk. A woman in a large red hat is blowing her nose. A man in a heavy overcoat is trying to remove it without making any noise. Part of me wants to say, "It's okay. Take your coat off. It's hot in here. I'll wait." But I don't. I continue with my story.

"And so, when I was eleven, I was placed in the Susquehanna Valley Home, in the care of Mr. McPherson and the people who worked there. It was hard sometimes, being a Home kid, but now those days are almost over."

This is where I launch into the "send me to college" bit. Geez, I hate this. My mouth keeps talking as my mind soars up and over the crowd.

I finish and Mac stands, applauding with the audience. I return to the folding chair, and Mac takes the podium again to make the pitch.

"I brought something with me," he says as he puts his hand on the shelf under the top of the podium. "Having heard Sue's story, I hope you'll help me fill it."

He pulls out an old battered felt hat. It's charcoal gray, soft and squashed, like it's been worn for many years. It makes me think of old men who live on the streets.

"It's my attention-getter, Sue," Mac explained to me. "I want people to realize they should put their money in the hat like they would in a collection plate."

He walks toward the audience, hat extended, and waits at the edge of the stage. Finally a gray-haired man who reminds me of Les comes up from the front row and takes the hat. As it moves from hand to hand, I sit on the small metal chair with my knees together, hands folded, eyes down. I want to disappear.

"Mac," I ask later, "have you ever passed the hat before?"

"Not really," he answers. By now we're driving home through the June evening. My window is open. The air is cool.

"How do you feel, asking strangers for money?"

"Oh gosh, Sue, I've had to do that all my life. But I've never done it quite this way. Or for quite this reason." He drives slowly through the night, talking about his work and how he's always having to ask for money from one group or another to keep the Home going.

We pass houses with porches and porch lights.

"How much did we collect tonight?" I feel greedy asking, but I want to know.

"$182 and some change."

"Some change?"

"Not everybody who belongs to the Lions or the Elks is rich, Sue," Mac says.

The hat sits on the seat between us. I try not to feel bad that people who don't have much money gave us some anyway.

"It's getting close to when we have to send in the first payment, isn't it?"

"Yup. Two months."

"How many more times do we do this?"

"Eight."

I turn and stare out the window.

Arranging the pieces

"What does it mean," I ask, "when a father I can't even remember sends me a present?"

Miss Maude and I are sitting in our usual chairs in the cottage living room having our good-night cigarettes. I am in a rigid wooden frame creation with an orange plastic seat. Miss Maude is leaning back in the well-worn overstuffed lounger she favors, rocking gently back and forth. Her pack of Kools is on the little end table between us.

"Do you think about him a lot?" she asks.

"Now I do. Every time I look at this watch, I think about him."

I take a drag on the Kool I bummed from Miss Maude.

"Did Mac tell you? Your father might be sending you a little money to help out while you're in college." She sounds like she's not a hundred percent sure about this.

"Yeah. Mac told me." I think about it. "He says there's going to be a go-between." This embarrasses me. Why doesn't my father want to be associated with me?

I tell her the rest of what I know. "It's a man who runs an insurance business in Chattanooga. Mac said my father will give this man some money and then Seth—that's his name—will send it to me."

Talking about this makes me want to move around. I cross the living room and look out the window. The streetlight at the end of our little sidewalk glows in the night.

"It's pretty strange, don't you think?" I ask her. "Why can't my father just send the money to me?"

I come back to my chair.

"You know, Sue, getting money from a go-between is no more difficult than telling your life's story to a room full of strangers and passing the hat." She smiles and leans over to brush my bangs out of my eyes.

I tap the end of my cigarette on the edge of the ashtray. The gold watch glows in the dim light.

"Do you understand why there has to be a go-between?" she asks, her voice quiet.

What does she know?

"No, I don't. Why?"

"Well, you know your father has remarried."

I nod. "Mac told me." My eyes are locked on Miss Maude's face.

"I don't know why, but your father's wife doesn't want him to have any contact with you." She shakes her pack of Kools until another cigarette appears. She pauses to light it. "So he decided to find someone else to send you the money."

I lean my head against the back of my chair and close my eyes. I thought a door to my dad had opened and now it's closing.

"Why doesn't she want him to have 'contact' with me, whatever that means?"

"I don't know, Sue."

When Miss Maude speaks again, it's to change the subject. "What about your mom, Sue? Will you miss her when you're away at school?"

Now I have to think about the other side of my so-called family. It's deep-breath time.

I decide to tell Miss Maude. "It's so hard when I see her. We both cry a lot. Sometimes, I get so nervous, I go into her bathroom and throw up." Miss Maude nods like she's not surprised.

"Did she ask you about the watch?"

"No. She hardly notices anything anymore. When I see her, I feel like I'm in a boat and she's still on the shore. Is that crazy?"

Miss Maude leans across the little end table and drapes her arm across my shoulders. She rocks us gently back and forth, like we're on a porch swing.

"You know, Sue, when you made Mac your legal guardian, it was the right thing to do. It would have been too much for your mom, trying to help you get into Bennington. All that paperwork." She shakes her head.

I take another deep breath and close my eyes. I'm about to confess something really bad.

"I never told Mom about the guardian thing."

"That's okay, dear. There's no reason for her to know." Miss Maude rubs my arm.

"I let her down." I am crying now. "I shouldn't have done that."

"Oh no, honey. That's simply not true." Miss Maude sits up straight and reaches for my chin. She tilts my wet face up and looks into my eyes.

"You took care of her, Sue. That's what you did. Mac and I know that. You mustn't think otherwise."

I lean back. My breathing slows. Except for the hall light, the living room is in darkness.

"Do you think I should send my father a thank you note?"

"That would be good." Her cigarette has burned out in the ashtray.

"What should I say?"

She thinks about it. "Just say thank you."

I sit up straight. "If he doesn't want any contact with me, where do I send it?"

"Mac has an address for the go-between. For Seth."

I think about that.

"Do I call my father 'Dad?'"

"What else would you call him?"

I think some more.

"Sue, honey, whatever you say is going to be fine. After all, he's going to get a note from his daughter, like you got one from him. You know, he's probably as nervous as you are about all this."

"I guess." But I'm still not sure.

I stub out my cigarette and kiss Miss Maude on the cheek. I start down the hallway toward my room. I am almost to the stairs when I hear, "I love you, Sue. You'll always be my bright penny."

"I love you, too, Miss Maude."

ON MY WAY

Getting ready

"**S**ue! I heard from Bennington."

It's August. We've been expecting to hear from them, but it's still a bit of a heart-stopper when Mac calls to tell me.

"And?"

"Congratulations! You're going to get a . . . wait a minute, let me find my note . . . a Jessie Smith Noyes Foundation grant. Plus you get to wait on tables *and* be a guide for prospective students so you'll have two jobs this year as well. Hey! Congratulations again, kiddo. You're now officially a Bennington College freshman!"

I can't answer through the tears.

The next day, we go to the bank and practically zero out my savings account. Then we send a check to Bennington for our half. Boy, I sure need those two jobs.

It's September. I'm leaving in less than a week. I feel like I'm about to do a "hit and run" down a very steep hill.

I walk around the Home, thinking about what it was like here when I was eleven. Or thirteen. Or fifteen. I sit on the bench where Mac and I sat and talked before I went to Florida. It's an old wooden bench, still sturdy. I'd like a cigarette, but I don't smoke on the grounds, except occasionally in the cottage with Miss Maude.

Yesterday was my last day at Ozalid. Fay doesn't work there any more either. "Too boring," she announced. She started dating some new guy, and they took off for some town in western Pennsylvania. I don't remember where.

The women in Accounts Receivable had a little good-bye party for me. We stood around holding paper cups of punch and eating cupcakes with sprinkles on them.

"Good luck, Sue," they said.

"Take it easy."

"Work hard and get good grades."

"Stay away from those college boys."

"You can do it, kid."

Stuff like that. In a funny way, I'll miss them.

I walk past the Main Building toward the Gym. It's usually empty around supper time. Inside, I turn on the overhead lights. The maintenance guys must have waxed the floor, it's so very shiny. Basketball hoops hang at each end of the space. I smile as I remember learning to play full-court basketball and the joy of running, dribbling the ball, the whole length of the court. Not many rules to the games we played here. Sort of a free-for-all, actually. But it was always the Home team vs. the Home team anyway, so it never really mattered.

I sit cross-legged on the shiny Gym floor and think about my first Christmas here. The huge tree—a real one—with all the presents stacked around it. I remember my "Girl, age 12" present. It turned out to be an angora sweater. I loved it. Wore it till the angora was flat as a pancake. Miss Maude said I should throw it away, but I kept it and wore it as a pajama top until it fell apart.

I want to slow everything down. I want to remember all that was said here at the Home, all that I did.

I go outside the Gym and look down the hill at the vegetable garden. When I was younger, I thought it went on for miles, but it's only a few acres. I think about the time those girls went out my bedroom window and ran away . . . .

"Sue, is that you?"

Mac calls to me from the stairs outside the Main Building. It's dusk. He's closing up for the night.

"Yeah. Just wandering around," I holler back. I start toward him. Mac waits for me by the sign that says, "Susquehanna Valley Children's Home." I think about the first time I saw it the morning after the fire.

"It's nice here this time of year, don't you think?" he asks.

"Yeah. I'll miss this place, I guess."

"Sue, you won't have time to miss the Home. You'll be too busy being a college freshman." He's trying to sound jolly.

"They got the money we sent, right?" I've already asked him this half a dozen times.

"You know they did. You're all set."

"So I have a room and everything?"

Mac smiles and nods. He knows part of me is afraid that I'll get there and they won't know who I am, that there won't be a place for me, that I won't belong there. He takes my arm, and we walk together toward the cottage.

Good-bye party

"Go back upstairs and wait in the living room. And don't come down until I call you!"

I can tell Miss Maude is frustrated. Earlier, I showed up as the girls were hanging crepe-paper streamers from the ceiling in the rec room. When I poked my head in the kitchen, Miss Maude was taking a big sheet cake out of the oven. I smile and go upstairs to wait for my "surprise" good-bye party.

I hear running feet as the girls dash between the kitchen and the rec room. Their giggles make me smile. They're so much younger than I am, and younger by far than the rough girls who were at the Home when I first arrived. I'm like the older sister now. Boy, the whole nature of this place has changed.

Finally I hear, "Sue, can you come downstairs for a minute, please?"

I begin to walk down the hallway to the stairs. I wonder where Mac is, and whether any of the other housemothers will be here. I wonder when I'll see this house again.

"Surprise!"

I stop in the doorway. Blue and white streamers stretch from the center of the ceiling to the walls and the corners. The red concrete floor is extra shiny. I cleaned this floor most Saturdays for what feels like a lot of years, scrubbing the old wax off with steel wool and then putting on a new coat. It's someone else's job now.

The room is filled with girls jumping up and down. Miss Maude stands behind them next to the sliding door that leads to the grounds. Mac is beside her, wearing the widest grin I've ever seen him wear. Miss Hartford is laughing and clapping, nodding at me with an "I knew you'd make it" look. Miss Rosa is there too, even though she chided me for years, telling me I'd "never finish high school, let alone go to college." She smiles around the room, not meeting my eyes.

They'd brought one of the rectangular folding tables in from the dining room to hold the cake and soft drinks. I walk toward the table, looking at the candles lit as though for a birthday. The icing is white with blue wiggles along the edge. In the middle, Miss Maude has written in deep pink, "To Sue on her way to Bennington!" I have a terrible feeling someone is going to yell, "Speech! Speech!" Thankfully no one does.

Miss Maude pushes up the sleeves of her cardigan and begins to cut the cake.

"First piece is for Sue," I hear one of the girls call. That piece of cake shows up in front of me on a paper plate held by little Jennie, who's twelve. Her eyes are shining. I smile at her and take the plate.

Someone bangs on a glass to get our attention. I hear Mac's voice.

"Okay, gang, let's have a little order here."

Laughter.

"It's our time to wish Sue a safe journey to Bennington, and a wonderful year there as a freshman."

Eyes are on me. Wide blue eyes, small dark eyes, wet shiny eyes. We are celebrating something none of us fully understands.

"We're very proud of you, Sue. Congratulations. And don't forget to write."

More laughter.

I hear a scraping sound. I turn to see two girls pushing and pulling a large box across the red concrete floor. It's covered in a mixture of paper—some shiny red, some with Christmas angels, some with birthday candles. I can tell the younger girls were in charge of wrapping. They stop in front of me, guarding their box like sentinels.

"This is for you, Sue," says Mary Ann, who is the older and taller of the two. Her straight black hair touches her shoulders, her bangs drop almost to her eyes. "We wrapped it."

"It's beautiful," I tell her, and I mean it.

"Open it, Sue, open it!" Jennie's taking the paper plate from me now so both my hands are free.

I pull apart the paper, which doesn't take long. There's a large cardboard box labeled Samsonite. Inside the box, I find the one thing I truly need. A suitcase. I tap the tough gray-blue plastic that forms its outside and nod with approval. Then I open the suitcase. The inside is covered in a pale blue silky lining with shallow pockets along the back and sides. There are straps with little buckles to hold things in place. It is sturdy and beautiful. There's a name tag attached to the handle where one of the girls has printed my name. The address part is blank.

I look over at Miss Maude, who is softly crying. She opens her arms to me and I step in. My tears dampen her shoulder. Mac reaches over and squeezes my hand.

"Thank you," I say. "I'll miss you all so much." My voice is so soft, I'm not sure anyone hears me.

The bus station

There's a dream I have over and over. I'm in the wings of a theater about to go on stage and I'm terrified. I don't know the lines, the blocking, when I'm supposed to enter and exit, nothing. I don't even know my character's name. My heart is racing so fast, I think I'm going to faint. Then suddenly, there I am on stage, sweating in the hot lights. I open my mouth and somehow the lines come out and I begin to act my role.

I feel like I'm in that dream now.

I am leaving. I am no longer a Home kid. I don't live anywhere. I have a headache.

Mac and I enter the waiting room, and the door to the bus station closes behind us. It smells like cheap tobacco and burned coffee. Even though it's morning, the waiting room is dim. Everything is in shadow. Mac came along to see me off. He helps me find the end of the ticket line. He sets my new gray-blue suitcase carefully on the floor between us.

As we wait, Mac reminds me that the bus stops at a lot of little towns between Binghamton and Bennington.

"I'm afraid it's going to take about six hours for you to get there," he says.

"That's okay," I tell him, smiling. "I like looking out the window."

A girl not much older than I am sits on a bench in the waiting room, her chin resting on her chest like she is sleeping. She has on a loose dress and comfortable shoes. That's probably what I should be wearing, but I'm not. I have on my new navy and green plaid skirt that makes a perfect circle when you spread it out on the ground. On top, I have a long-sleeved white cotton blouse ironed last night by Miss Maude while we said our good-byes.

The line inches forward.

"What if I don't make it in time?"

"They're not going to let the bus leave without you, Sue." Mac is smiling at me, his eyes twinkling in a way that tells me, "Everything is going to be all right." I know this, but I can't stop worrying.

"Remember, Sue, when you get to Bennington, there will be taxis at the bus station. You get in one and tell the driver to take you to Franklin House at the college." Mac waits for me to nod. I've never been in a taxi.

"And don't hesitate to call if you need anything. Remember, Jean and I will be up in two weeks and we can bring things." The phone number for Mac's office is burned into my brain.

We arrive at the ticket window. Mac steps aside.

"One ticket to Bennington, Vermont, please," I say to the woman with tired eyes behind the counter.

"Round trip?"

I look at Mac.

He nods.

"Yes, please."

I pull out my wallet. I give her the money and take the ticket.

Mac picks up my suitcase and we go out to the boarding area. It's a chilly concrete tunnel. There's a strong smell of fuel. We find the sign that says "Bennington, Vermont" and take our place at the end of that line.

"Mac?"

"Yes, Sue?" He pats his pockets, then pulls out a large white handkerchief and blows his nose.

"Nothing."

"You know, Sue, when we come up to see you, it would be great if you showed me around. We've only seen the campus covered in snow, remember?" We both smile, thinking about our visit back in March.

The Greyhound bus pulls to a stop beside us, and the door opens with a whoosh. The driver slides out from behind the wheel and climbs down the steps to the waiting area.

"Bennington and points in between," he calls.

The line moves quickly now. People pile their luggage next to the bus, hand the driver their tickets, and disappear inside. I pick up my shiny new suitcase and place it carefully next to the growing stack of bags and boxes.

Everything around me begins to fade. I look at Mac. It's like I'm already seeing him through the window as we pull away.

I hand the driver my ticket. He checks it and tears it in half, giving me back the return portion. Then he grins at Mac.

"Going away to school, is she?"

"Yes indeed," Mac answers. "She certainly is."

Bennington College seeks students with intellectual vitality and inherent curiosity—a kind of creative restlessness that cuts across backgrounds and experiences. It is our hope and our aim that in their four years at Bennington students discover and set a course for a most remarkable life's work. Susan Pickering DuMond '63 did just that, and we are pleased to have played a role in the unfolding of her story.

— Janet Lape Marsden,
Former Vice President, Bennington College

ACKNOWLEDGMENTS

There are many who supported me during the creation of this book. First, a significant thank you to my writers group led by Shoshana Alexander and comprised of a talented and constructive circle: Deedie Runkel, Carol Hwoschinsky, Carolyn Shaffer and Pam Derby. Their attention to my story and to the writer were critical in completing *Another Place Called Home.* My thanks also to friends who read and encouraged my work—Barbara Cole, Charlene Setlow, Livia Genise, Steve and Judith Auerbach, Judi Stratton, Blair Ritchie, Barbara Thacker among others. I am also grateful to Molly Best Tinsley, author, professor, and cofounder of Fuze Publishing, for her thoughts regarding this evasive thing called writing.

Special thanks to *Fish Anthology 2013* for including "The Visit" as one of the top ten short memoirs to appear in their publication. It was a valuable encouragement. Also my thanks to WOW-WomenOnWriting for awarding an Honorable Mention to a fictionalized version of "The Hat."

Enduring gratitude goes to my family, a word I didn't begin to comprehend during my childhood but one which is so important to me now. To my husband, Robert Armen, who supported and applauded me during this lengthy process and to my stepson, Aaron, and my daughter-in-law, Veronica. My family provided a loving presence as I wrote my story.

My eternal thanks to my mentors, John F. McPherson known as Mac, the Home's director, and to Mrs. Maude McMaster known as Miss Maude, the loving widow who became my housemother. They supported and guided me during my six years at the Home. Through them, I found my strength and my path.

Finally, I extend special thanks to Bennington College, Bennington, Vermont for reaching out to Sue Pickering, a foster kid, as she struggled to escape her uneven and difficult past. Bennington College is clear and strong in its purpose regarding its students, including the College's desire to "enlarge, deepen and transform their lives." Thanks to Bennington for helping me put the pieces back together.